First World War
and Army of Occupation
War Diary
France, Belgium and Germany

40 DIVISION
Divisional Troops
224 Field Company Royal Engineers
1 June 1916 - 30 April 1919

WO95/2600/1

The Naval & Military Press Ltd
www.nmarchive.com
Published in association with The National Archives

Published by

The Naval & Military Press Ltd

Unit 10 Ridgewood Industrial Park,

Uckfield, East Sussex,

TN22 5QE England

Tel: +44 (0) 1825 749494

www.naval-military-press.com

www.nmarchive.com

This diary has been reprinted in facsimile from the original. Any imperfections are inevitably reproduced and the quality may fall short of modern type and cartographic standards.

© **Crown Copyright**
Images reproduced by permission of The National Archives, London, England, 2015.

Contents

Document type	Place/Title	Date From	Date To
Heading	WO95/2600/1		
Heading	40th Division 224th Field Coy R.E. Jun 1916-Apr 1919		
War Diary		01/06/1916	30/06/1916
Heading	War Diary of 224th Field Coy. R.E. From 1st July 1916 to 31st July 1916 40 July 224 Fere Vol 2		
War Diary		01/07/1916	31/07/1916
Heading	War Diary of 224th (Field) Coy. R.E. From Aug 1st 1916 to Aug 31st 1916 Volume 3		
War Diary		01/08/1916	31/08/1916
Heading	War Diary 224th (Field) Company R.E. September 1916 From Sept 1st 1916 to Sept. 30th 1916 Volume 4		
War Diary		01/09/1916	30/09/1916
War Diary	War Diary 224th Field Coy. R.E. Oct. 1st 1916 Oct 31st 1916 Vol V		
War Diary	Les Brebis	01/10/1916	31/10/1916
Heading	War Diary 224th Field Company R.E. November, 1916 Volume VI		
Heading	D.A.G., 3rd Echelon. 224 Fere Vol 5	05/11/1916	05/11/1916
War Diary	On the March	01/11/1916	14/11/1916
War Diary	Coigneux	14/11/1916	30/11/1916
Heading	War Diary of 224th Field Coy. R.E. December, 1916 Volume VII		
War Diary	Le Toile	01/12/1916	10/12/1916
War Diary	Maorepas	11/12/1916	25/12/1916
War Diary	Le Forest	26/12/1916	31/12/1916
Heading	War Diary of 224th Field Company R.E. Month of January 1917 Volume VIII		
War Diary	Le Forest	01/01/1917	31/01/1917
Heading	224 Rd Coy Vol 9 A.F. 2118 War Diary February 1917 Vol. 9		
War Diary	Camp 14	01/02/1917	28/02/1917
Heading	War Diary of 224th Field Coy. R.E. From 1st March 1917 to 31st March 1917 Volume 10		
War Diary	Camp 14 (Old Site)	01/03/1917	01/03/1917
War Diary	Prisoners Camp	02/03/1917	05/03/1917
War Diary	Camp 161	06/03/1917	06/03/1917
War Diary	Clery	07/03/1917	31/03/1917
Heading	War Diary Vol XI. 224th (Field) Company R.E. April. 1917		
War Diary	Clery	01/04/1917	06/04/1917
War Diary	Fins	07/04/1917	30/04/1917
Heading	224th Field Coy. R.E. War Diary From:- 1st May 1917 to 31st May 1917 Volume 12		
War Diary Miscellaneous	Fins	01/05/1917	02/05/1917
War Diary Miscellaneous	Fins	03/05/1917	31/05/1917
Miscellaneous	Headquarters 119th Infantry Brigade Report of Operation on L.A. Vacquerie	06/05/1917	06/05/1917
Heading	War Diary 224th Field Co. R.E. Vol 13 June 1917		

Heading	??		
War Diary	Fins	01/06/1917	30/06/1917
Heading	War Diary 224th Field, Co. R.E. July 1917 Vol 14		
War Diary	Heudecourt	01/07/1917	31/07/1917
Heading	War Diary of 224th Field Coy. R.E. From 1st August 1917 to 31st August 1917 Volume 15		
War Diary	Heudecourt	01/08/1917	31/08/1917
War Diary	War Diary of 224th Field Coy. R.E.F From:- 1st Sept. 1917 to 30th Sept. 1917 Vol No. 16		
War Diary	Heudecourt	01/09/1917	30/09/1917
Heading	War Diary of 224th Field Company. R.E. From 1st October 1917 to:- 31st October 1917 Volume 17		
War Diary	Heudecourt	01/10/1917	18/10/1917
War Diary	Peronne	19/10/1917	19/10/1917
War Diary	Larbret.	20/10/1917	29/10/1917
War Diary	Peronne	30/10/1917	30/10/1917
War Diary	Equancourt	31/10/1917	20/11/1917
War Diary	Rocquiny	21/11/1917	21/11/1917
War Diary	Beaumetz	22/11/1917	22/11/1917
War Diary	Havrincourt	23/11/1917	30/11/1917
Heading	War Diary of 224th Field Coy. R.E. From 1st Decr. 1917 to 31st Decr. 1917 Volume No. 19		
War Diary	Havrincourt	01/12/1917	04/12/1917
War Diary	Boiry Becquerelle	04/12/1917	29/12/1917
War Diary	Ervillers	30/12/1917	31/12/1917
Heading	War Diary of 224th Field Company R.E. From:- 1st January 1918 to:- 31st January 1918 Volume 20		
War Diary	Ervillers	01/01/1918	01/01/1918
War Diary	Noreuil	02/01/1918	31/01/1918
Heading	224th Field Co. R.E. War Diary Vol 21		
War Diary	Noreuil	01/02/1918	10/02/1918
War Diary	Hamlincourt	11/02/1918	28/02/1918
Heading	40th Divisional Engineers War Diary 224th Field Company R.E. March 1918		
War Diary	Bailleul Mont	01/03/1918	12/03/1918
War Diary	Hendecourt	12/03/1918	18/03/1918
War Diary	Hendecourt Armrgh Camp Hamlincourt. Gomiecourt	21/03/1918	25/03/1918
War Diary	Monchy-au-bois	26/03/1918	26/03/1918
War Diary	Bienvillers	27/03/1918	27/03/1918
War Diary	Sombrin.	28/03/1918	29/03/1918
War Diary	Orlencourt	30/03/1918	30/03/1918
War Diary	Rue Provost	31/03/1918	31/03/1918
War Diary	Ecquedecques	31/03/1918	31/03/1918
Miscellaneous	At 8p.m. the 21st March 1918 the Company was in No. 6 Camp. Hendecourt.	27/03/1918	27/03/1918
Heading	40th Divisional Engineer. War Diary 224th Field Company R.E. April 1918		
Heading	War Diary (Vol.23) April 1918 (1st-30th) 224 Field Coy. R.E.		
War Diary	Fort Rompu H.7.d (Sheet 36)	01/04/1918	09/04/1918
War Diary	Neuf Berquin	10/04/1918	10/04/1918
War Diary	Merris	10/04/1918	10/04/1918
War Diary	Laverrier	10/04/1918	11/04/1918
War Diary	Strazeele	12/04/1918	12/04/1918
War Diary	Hondeghem	13/04/1918	13/04/1918
War Diary	Cormette	14/04/1918	20/04/1918

War Diary	Zuytpeene	21/04/1918	21/04/1918
War Diary	Hardifort	22/04/1918	22/04/1918
War Diary	J 25.b. 3.8. (Sheet 27)	23/04/1918	24/04/1918
War Diary	Hardifort	25/04/1918	30/04/1918
Heading	War Diary of 224 Field Company, R.E. May 1st 1918 to May 31st 1918 Volume 23		
War Diary	Hardifort	01/05/1918	01/05/1918
War Diary	J.25.b.3.8 (Sheet 27 Belgium & Part of France)	01/05/1918	11/05/1918
War Diary	Hardifort	12/05/1918	31/05/1918
Heading	War Diary of 224 Field Company. R.E. June 1st 1918-June 30th 1918 Volume 25		
War Diary	Hardifort J. 25.b.3.8. (Sheet 27)	01/06/1918	03/06/1918
War Diary	Balemberg H.33.b.5.6 (Sheet 27)	04/06/1918	16/06/1918
War Diary	Balemberg	22/06/1918	23/06/1918
War Diary	Wallon Cappel 11.18.d.5.5	23/06/1918	30/06/1918
Heading	War Diary of 224 Field Company, R.E. From 1st July 1918 to 31st July 1918 Volume 26		
War Diary	Wallon Cappel (11.18.d.5.5 Sheet 27)	01/07/1918	06/07/1918
War Diary	Eecke (Q.25.d.9.9 Sheet 27)	11/07/1918	31/07/1918
Heading	War Diary 224th Field Company. R.E. From August 1st. 1918 to August 31st 1918 Volume 27		
War Diary	Eecke. Q.25.d.9.9 Sheet 27	01/08/1918	23/08/1918
War Diary	Hazebrouck Garage	24/08/1918	25/08/1918
War Diary	D.5.c.9.1. Sheet 36 A	25/08/1918	26/08/1918
War Diary	Sanitas Corner	27/08/1918	27/08/1918
War Diary	E.15.c.65.60	28/08/1918	29/08/1918
War Diary	Sanitas Corner	29/08/1918	31/08/1918
Heading	War Diary of 224 Field Company, R.E. From:-1st Sept. 1918. to:- 30th Sept.1918. Volume 28		
War Diary	Sanitas Corner	01/09/1918	01/09/1918
War Diary	E15.c 65 60/36a	02/09/1918	03/09/1918
War Diary	Noute Boom	04/09/1918	04/09/1918
War Diary	36A/F.17.a.2.8	05/09/1918	08/09/1918
War Diary	36/A.18.d.3.3	09/09/1918	13/09/1918
War Diary	A.18.d.3.3	13/09/1918	26/09/1918
War Diary	36/A.18.d.3.3	27/09/1918	30/09/1918
Heading	War Diary of 224 Field Company. R.E. From:- 1st Oct.1918 to:- 31st Oct. 1918 Volume 29		
War Diary	A.18.d.3.3 (Sheet 36)	01/10/1918	01/10/1918
War Diary	W. Steenwerck.	01/10/1918	05/10/1918
War Diary	A. 8.d.3.3	06/10/1918	15/10/1918
War Diary	B.30.c.14	16/10/1918	18/10/1918
War Diary	J.8.d.65.05	19/10/1918	19/10/1918
War Diary	Perenchies	20/10/1918	22/10/1918
War Diary	K.2.b.8.0	23/10/1918	23/10/1918
War Diary	Wambrechies	23/10/1918	24/10/1918
War Diary	36.5.26.b.8.0	25/10/1918	26/10/1918
War Diary	Lys-Lez-Lannoy	27/10/1918	27/10/1918
War Diary	37/g/4.d.8.2	28/10/1918	31/10/1918
Heading	224 Field Coy. R.E. Nov. 1918 Vol: 30 War Diary		
Heading	Capt. Grantham, 224th Field Coy. R.E.		
War Diary	Lys-Lez-Lannoy 37/G.4.d.8.2	01/11/1918	09/11/1918
War Diary	Petit Lannoy (Near Pecq)	10/11/1918	10/11/1918
War Diary	C.25.d. 1.1	11/11/1918	20/11/1918
War Diary	Herinnes 37/C.21.b.58	21/11/1918	30/11/1918

Heading	War Diary 224 Field Company, R.E. From:- 1st Dec. 1918 To:- 31st Dec. 1918 Volume No. 31		
War Diary	Herinnes 37/C.21.b.5.8	01/12/1918	01/12/1918
War Diary	Petit Baisseux	02/12/1918	31/12/1918
Heading	War Diary of 224 Field Coy. R.E. From:- 1st Jan 1919. To:- 31st Jan 1919 Volume 32		
War Diary	Petit Baisieux. 37/m.17.d.7.6	01/01/1919	28/01/1919
War Diary	Croix	29/01/1919	29/01/1919
War Diary	36/L.9.b.05.25	30/01/1919	31/01/1919
Heading	War Diary 224 Field Company. R.E. February 1919 Vol.29		
War Diary	Croix 36/L.9.b.05.25	01/02/1919	28/02/1919
Heading	224th Field Co. R.E. War Diary March 1919. Vol.34		
War Diary	Croix 36/L 9.b.05.25	01/03/1919	19/03/1919
War Diary	Croix	20/03/1919	31/03/1919
War Diary	224th Field Co. R.E. War Diary March 1919 Apl Vol 35		
War Diary	Croix 36/L.9.b.05.25	01/04/1919	30/04/1919

W0095/2600/1

40TH DIVISION

224TH FIELD COY R.E.
JUN 1916 – APR 1919

WAR DIARY
or
INTELLIGENCE SUMMARY

Army Form C. 2118

224th Coy R E

Jun '16
Apr '19

Place	Date	Hour	Summary of Events and Information	Remarks and references to Appendices
	1/6/16		224th Coy 6 Officers & 223 OR left Pirbright and entrained in two Great trainloads for Southampton. The Coy entrained all horses & wheeled transport. 3 Officers & 96 OR on one boat. Remainder on another boat. The Coy disembarked at HAVRE & marched to HALLE III "Rue Mte" bivouacs on the stone floor until 3/6/16	
	3/6/16		The Coy entrained at HAVRE took 6 at 1915 & proceeded via ABBEVILLE (where horses were watered & breakfasts served) to LILLERS.	
	4/6/16		The Coy detrained at LILLERS at 1100 & marched to LIGNY LES AIRE. They were billeted in farms. Officers were all in Chateau.	
	4/6/16		Coy remained billeted at LIGNY. The weather was very hot & the hot days occupied in Route marches & harness.	
	12/6/16		The dismounted personnel were brought in motor busses to NOYELLES arriving at 1400 for attachment to 15th Divn for training & were accomodated in huts. The mounted men with all horses & wagons sent by march route to SAILLY LABOURSE. There was no accomodation & shelters were erected using tarpaulins & tarpaulins. 27 NOYELLES ROAD	
	13/6/16		The Coy before work on 6 days Supports in Redoubt line Rt Divisional continuously carried out in 4 reliefs 2330, 1100, 1700, 2300, 50 infantry being employed for each shift.	

WAR DIARY or INTELLIGENCE SUMMARY

(Erase heading not required.)

Army Form C. 2118

Place	Date	Hour	Summary of Events and Information	Remarks and references to Appendices
	20/6		20 Sappers & 2 N.C.Os started, under 9/54 7d Coy, laying tram lines & continued nightly.	
	21/6		The R.E. & Sappers on dugouts was reduced to 20 on each shift & work was begun on dismantling & rebuilding of Reserve line, the first rear priority. Two parties of 25 daily.	
	22/6		2 Snipers priority.	
	16/6		Three casualties occurred, 1 man being killed & 1 wounded in front line by shell fire coming from work trench mortar. One man was wounded by shell fire coming from work.	
	22/6 10th 23/6	}	Work continued on dugouts and laying of tram lines. Since 9/04 Tuesday R.E. Work on Reserve line continued but no by available.	
	26/6 27/6		Heavy working under 9/04 Tuesday by orders of C.R.E. 15th Division R.E. Drill parades, kit inspections etc.	
	28/6		Coy moved by march route to RUITZ. The weather was very bad. The transport marched independently. Coy went into billets in RUITZ. Two sections accommodated in large empty building. Remainder by half sections in barns & lofts. Horses all under cover, mules in picket lines.	
	29/6		Fatigues & drills — weather fine — Officers reconnoitred crater at Sclanty Mines NOEUX LES MINES.	

WAR DIARY
~~INTELLIGENCE SUMMARY~~
(Erase heading not required.)

Army Form C. 2118

Instructions regarding War Diaries and Intelligence Summaries are contained in F.S. Regs., Part II. and the Staff Manual respectively. Title Pages will be prepared in manuscript.

Place	Date	Hour	Summary of Events and Information	Remarks and references to Appendices
30/1/16			Work commenced on CRATER at NOEUX LES MINES. Two sections working 4 hour shift in morning, 2 sects 4 hour shift in afternoon.	

R. Collins
Capt.
O.C. 224 Coy RE

30/1/16.

40 July
224 F R E
Vol 2

War Diary
of
224th Field Coy R.E.

from 1st July 1916 to 31st July 1916.

Army Form C. 2118

WAR DIARY
or
INTELLIGENCE SUMMARY
(Erase heading not required.)

Instructions regarding War Diaries and Intelligence Summaries are contained in F.S. Regs., Part II. and the Staff Manual respectively. Title Pages will be prepared in manuscript.

Place	Date	Hour	Summary of Events and Information	Remarks and references to Appendices
	1916 July 1st		Company in Billets at RUITZ. Work continued on trades came parties as previously. Small party sent to repair shed at Anne fas Donne.	
	" 2nd		Orders received for Company to move on July 3rd to take over Billets from 107 Lowland Field Company for Work in MAROC SECTOR with 121st Brigade. Officer Commanding with one Officer proceeded to C.R.E 109 Division at NOEUX LES MINES and proceeded to LES BREBIS returning after seeing Billets etc.	
	" 3rd		Company proceeded by march route to LES BREBIS and were billeted there. Officers in a large unfurnished Estaminet – One Section and the remainder in Billets of rest character – reminder in Billets in ruins of GRENAY.	
	" 4th		Officer Commanding went round left Sub Sector with Y.O.C. Brigade. Officer N.B.O's reconnoitred trenches. Officer & 8 men started with Infantry party concerning crater.	
	" 5th		Officer Commanding went round right Sub Sector with Y.O.C. Principal work:- Communication of trader, repair to CRASSIER Trenches and with Infantry parties in repair of front support Trenches.	

Army Form C. 2118

WAR DIARY
or
INTELLIGENCE SUMMARY
(Erase heading not required.)

Instructions regarding War Diaries and Intelligence Summaries are contained in F. S. Regs., Part II. and the Staff Manual respectively. Title Pages. will be prepared in manuscript.

Place	Date	Hour	Summary of Events and Information	Remarks and references to Appendices
	1916 July 5		Shelled by enemy. Party of R.E. with 50 Infantry as escort repairing light railway. Weather very bad.	
	" 6		Work continued as above.	
	" 7		Work continued on light railway. Weather very heavy.	
	" 8th, " 9th		Work continued on front line trenches many of which had been badly knocked in by shell fire.	
	" 10th		Work as above.	
	" 11th, " 12th, " 13th, " 14th, " 15th		Railway system in order. Parties for projects to Barracons & Brigade taken up nightly to Barracons Headquarters. Other work as before.	
	" 16th, " 17th, " 18th		Work as before. Weather good. as above. Old trench opened up as PALL MALL for about 250'. Work as before.	

WAR DIARY or INTELLIGENCE SUMMARY

(Erase heading not required.)

Army Form C. 2118

Place	Date	Hour	Summary of Events and Information	Remarks and references to Appendices
	1916 July 19		Work as before. Crater consolidation completed.	
	" 20		Work as before. Railway running well. Raid by Right Battalion accompanied by 2 N.C.Os. R.E. and 2 Sappers. No reliefs. Sappers carried Ypres iron charges made up in case they were required for blowing up dug outs etc. Horse-Lines order - one driver no. 9920 & Madeline W. wounded and also Myers and one horse wounded.	
	" 21.		Work as before.	
	" 22.		nos 213 stations proceeded to LOOS and took over work of 156th Field Company. The work consists of conservation of three Mine Craters and also deep dug outs. All work S. of Route Tranerie was handed over to 231st Field Company R.E. Stations at LOOS are billeted in cellars. Remaining stations and Headquarters remain in GRENAY	
	" 23.		for work N. of Route Tranerie. Work continues as above.	
	" 24.		Work continues as above.	
	" 25.		Work at LOOS continues on deep dug outs and conservation of trenches. Work on Right Sector: deep dug outs in 2 WEEN STREET, blowing of	

WAR DIARY or INTELLIGENCE SUMMARY

Army Form C. 2118

Place	Date	Hour	Summary of Events and Information	Remarks and references to Appendices
	1916 July 25		Abandoned trenches and repair of trenches.	
	26 to 28th		Work as above. The trenches at the craters are being and repaired every night. Work on dugouts not interfered with and continuous reliefs of 8 hours maintained. No difficulty found in obtaining and transporting of stores to LOOS.	
	29		Two sections of 229th Field Coy R.E. attached to this Coy for work at LOOS. All 4 Battalions of Brigade now in line. Our sections allotted work in same area as Barracun. Other sections as work not directly connected with Barracun.	
	30		Work as above.	
	31			

R. [signature]
Major R.E.
Commanding 234th Field Coy. R.E.
July 31st/16

W+R

CONFIDENTIAL

WAR DIARY

of
228 (FIELD) Coy RE

from Aug 1st 1916 to Aug 21st 1916

VOLUME 3

Army Form C. 2118

WAR DIARY or INTELLIGENCE SUMMARY

(Erase heading not required.)

August 1916   254th Field Coy RE

Place	Date	Hour	Summary of Events and Information	Remarks and references to Appendices
	1916 Aug 1st		Two sections of Company with two sections of 229th field company attached at LOOS. One section working on R.E. work in Battalion area which consisted principally of deep dug-outs and consolidation of craters. The progress on SEAFORTH CRATER was slow as the enpr. were in full view of the enemy and were continually blown in. Two sections were working on Right sub-section renewing the support line and also making concreted stations for concealment in PALL MALL with deep dug-out. One officer and 48 Infantry permanently attached to Company for work. No.9924 L/Cpl Friday wounded by rifle grenade in front line trenches.	
	2nd to 4th		Work continued as above. Engine of light railway below stack of pann & salt up to aspano.	
	8th		After work on night of 7/8th the two sections from LOOS returned and the two sections of 229th Field Coy RE rejoined their company.	
	9th		Work carried on by two sections in MAROC SECTOR.	
	10th		The Company took over its new line of MAROC SECTOR. Two sections working on North of craters and two South of craters	
	11th		Work as above	
	12th		- do -	
	13th		- do -	

WAR DIARY or INTELLIGENCE SUMMARY

(Erase heading not required.)

Army Form C. 2118

Place	Date	Hour	Summary of Events and Information	Remarks and references to Appendices
	1916 Aug 14		The following work was then in hand in this SECTOR:-	
			1 Medium Trench Mortar Emplacement	Queen Street.
			- do -	Cordiale Avenue.
			- do -	Jenny's Street.
			1 Stokes gun Emplacement.	Support Line.
			- do -	Tegenne Rd. Bay 3.
			- do -	Bay. 24.
			- do -	Cordiale Avenue.
				Queen Street.
				Sau Viger.
			1 Machine gun Emplacement.	
			Bay. with 1 – 2 face.	Tegenne – 3 Bay.
			" – 2 "	to Tegenne Rd.
			" – 2 "	New Rep.
			" – 2 "	10. B – 12.
			" – 2 "	15 – 16.
			" – 2 "	16 – 17.
			" – 2 "	Kinstone Street
			" – 2 enlarging	Victoria Alley.
			" – 2 face	Cordiale Avenue.
			" – 3 face	St James Rep.
			" – 2 "	Sau Viger.
			" – 2 "	Sau Vieu.
				Traverse Road. Bay. 22.
			1 Heavy Trench Mortar Emplacement with Dug-out & Ammunition Store.	
			General Work. Sniper's posts in Right Sub Sector.	Repairof firesteps Cordiale Avenue.

WAR DIARY or INTELLIGENCE SUMMARY

Army Form C. 2118

(Erase heading not required.)

Instructions regarding War Diaries and Intelligence Summaries are contained in F.S. Regs., Part II. and the Staff Manual respectively. Title Pages. will be prepared in manuscript.

Place	Date	Hour	Summary of Events and Information	Remarks and references to Appendices
	Aug 14/16		General Works (Gorgas) Repairing fire-bay — do — Block sewers etc. Repair to Machine Gun 5. Constructing shelter for form pear in South More.	
			Contractors	
	15th		Machine Gun Emplacement on Caravan.	JD7
	16th		Work as above. Reinforcements (10) arrived from Base. Work as above. Temporary Lieut N.W. Pearson relieved by advising line in rear of front line.	JD7 JD7
	17th		Work continued as above. Dug out on TRAVERS ROAD completed & one on BOYAU 22 begun and also heavy trench Mortar Emplacement begun near NEUFALLEY. One officer & 26 men from 11th Royal Lancaster Regt. and 26 men from Highland Light Infantry temporarily attached for work.	JD7
	18th		Work as above.	JD7
	19th		— do — Dug out at St. to complete.	JD7 JD7
	20th		— do — Temporary 2nd Lt. Ya Clark arrived from Base.	JD7

WAR DIARY
INTELLIGENCE SUMMARY
(Erase heading not required.)

Army Form C. 2118

Place	Date	Hour	Summary of Events and Information	Remarks and references to Appendices
	Aug 21/6		Work continues as before. To 99.185 dappes of A Trenyor slightly manned by Rifle Grenades in front line trenches.	ADJ
	Aug 22		Work as before.	ADJ
	23		Men of 11th R. Irish Regt and Shepherds Light Infantry withdrawn.	ADJ
	24		Work as before.	ADJ
	25		do. Emplacements of Eng. and completed in PALL MALL.	ADJ
	26		100 Bangalores made up. — four were placed S. of Crateri and two N. of Craterii. Of the 6 only 5 were fired, as the infantry carrying 3 of 30 + 3 of 40 feet, the 6th torpedo. The Bangalores were not go through. The gaps cut were good but the infantry	ADJ
	28		Work as above. Three dug outs finished.	ADJ
	29		The fine spell of weather broke with torrential rains. The surface water flooded the trenches in MAROC. The communication trenches were very little damaged, but most of the support line was damaged and is now being repaired, improving its length.	ADJ
	30		The weather continues very stormy.	ADJ
	31		Work as above. New engine for light railway arrived	ADJ

A. Allen
Capt R.E.
Comdg 224th Fd Coy R.E.
Aug 31/16

Vol 4

Confidential

War Diary

224th (Field) Company R.E.

September 1916

From Sept 1st 1916 — To Sept 30th 1916

Volume 4

Army Form C. 2118

WAR DIARY
or
INTELLIGENCE SUMMARY
(Erase heading not required.)

Instructions regarding War Diaries and Intelligence Summaries are contained in F. S. Regs., Part II. and the Staff Manual respectively. Title Pages will be prepared in manuscript.

Place	Date	Hour	Summary of Events and Information	Remarks and references to Appendices
	1916 Sept 1st		Work on the following dug outs continued :- Boyau 3, Neuf Alley Keep, Edgeware Road Keep. Work on Support line & Boyau 6 in both but below continued. Trench Mortar Emplacements continued.	AP
	2nd		Reserve Support Line with trench elements from Edgeware Road to Liverpool Trench continued. Work on Support Gun Emplacements continued supporting Line Boyau 3.	AP
	3rd		All work continued as above.	AP
	4th		do - do.	AP
			One Officer + 25 men of 19th Royal Scots Regt. + 25 men of East Surrey Regiment attached for work on dug outs. Heavy trench mortar Emplacement completed in Neuf Alley in Garoc line.	AP
	5th		Trench work and trench mortar Emplacements continued. A small bombing intelligence in the southern branches. One N.C.O + one sapper took party No 99 + 2 sapper leading nightly movement from pipe line in front line trenches.	AP
	6th		Work continued as above. Dug out for garrison in St James Keep completed. Dug out at Neuf Alley Keep completed also dopes from Emplacement Boyau 3.	AP
	7th		Work continued as above. 2 Officers of 14th Highland Regt. of Infantry attached for work on dug outs.	AP

1875 Wt. W593/826 1,000,000 4/15 J.B.C. & A. A.D.S.S./Forms/C. 2118.

WAR DIARY
or
INTELLIGENCE SUMMARY

(Erase heading not required.)

Army Form C. 2118

Place	Date	Hour	Summary of Events and Information	Remarks and references to Appendices
	1916 Sept. 7th		Four Trench Mortar Emplacements right of Right Sub Sector completed. Other work continued. Party in Liverpool Street completed. Roof to Machine gun & emplacement continued.	A7
	8th		Two Trench Mortar Emplacements left of Right Sub-Sector completed. Other work continued.	A7
	9th		Work as above.	A7
	10th		do.	
	11th		Four Bryans completed. Tram line railway commenced. Very Avery to Rayenne Road. All work continued.	A7
			One Officer & 32 men of 3rd York (Pioneer) returned and attached to 229th Field Coy R.E. for work on Tops. Nine men attached to this Coy's workshop returned to units. Trench Mortar Emplacement, Cordiale Avenue, left Sub Sector completed. Dug outs in Bryans 6, 9 & 10 commenced.	
	12th		Work as above. Heavy Trench Mortar Emplacement completed. Gun placed in position and ready for action. Capt F.S. Green to O. Officer Commanding 224th Field Coy R.E. transferred to 1/2nd Infantry Brigade Headquarters, as Brigade Major.	A7
	13th		Work as above. Trench Mortar Emplacement Loredale Avenue, left of Sub-Sector completed.	A7

WAR DIARY
or
INTELLIGENCE SUMMARY
(Erase heading not required.)

Army Form C. 2118

Instructions regarding War Diaries and Intelligence Summaries are contained in F.S. Regs., Part II. and the Staff Manual respectively. Title Pages. will be prepared in manuscript.

Place	Date	Hour	Summary of Events and Information	Remarks and references to Appendices
	1916 April 14		Work continued. No. 9 & 20 Sappers & Obly accidentaly injured by face of earth in dug-out.	207
	15th		Work continued. Ammunition Bomb store construction Reference Road.	207
	16th		All work continued. 25 men of Argyle Sutherland Highlanders attached for work on dug-outs in Supply Line 2,3. Front Line revetting stopped.	207
	17th		Work as above. T.A.I. & Bomb Reserve Store completed Junction O.G.1 and Trench Street. Dug-out Enferme Road completed.	207
	18th		Work continued as above.	207
	19th		- do -	207
	20th		- do -	207
	21st		All men available for work on dug-outs detached.	207
			Work continued as above.	207
	22		- no -	
			One Officer & 24 men, 12th A.& S. Regt. 24 men of 19th R.W.F. & 25 men of 18th Welsh Regiment attached for work on dug-outs. One I.A.I. & Bomb Reserve Store complete at Junction Union Street & North Street.	207

WAR DIARY
or
INTELLIGENCE SUMMARY

Army Form C. 2118

(Erase heading not required.)

Place	Date	Hour	Summary of Events and Information	Remarks and references to Appendices
	1916 Sept 23rd		All work continued. Several sentry shelters to be erected in support line.	A/7
	" 24th		Work continued.	A/7
	" 25th		- do -	A/7
	" 26th		- do -	A/7
	" 27th		One N.C.O. & 20 men attached for work on two German Mortar Emplacements. Dug outs in Gorarde Avenue & Jermyn Street. Shelter at the back of traverses in front line started. One J.C.O. & 13 Bomb Reserve store completed Junction Jewish Street & Jermyn Street. Sentry boxes covered in front line completed.	A/7
	" 28th		Work continued. French Mortar Emplacements Jermyn Street finished. Deep dug off Freize Alley completed.	A/7
	" 29th		All work continued.	A/7
	" 30th		- do -	
			Capt. L.D. Miller from 110th Division took over command of the Company in place of Capt H.S. Cocuran who has been transferred to Brigade Headquarters.	A/7

T W Mully
Major R.E.
Commanding 22nd (W) Field Co. R.E.
Sept 30/9/16

CONFIDENTIAL
WAR DIARY
224th FIELD Coy RE
(Oct 31st 1916.
Vol X
(Oct 1st 1916 –

WAR DIARY or INTELLIGENCE SUMMARY

Army Form C. 2118

(Erase heading not required.)

Place	Date	Hour	Summary of Events and Information	Remarks and references to Appendices
LES BREBIS	1st		No 1 Section - Cleaning out existing trenches	
			No 2 Section - Three deep dugouts	
			No 3 Section - Cleaning out existing trenches, one deep dugout	TW 21
			No 4 Section - Cleaning out existing trenches, one deep dugout, one buit alone	
	2nd		As on 1st	TW 4
			One additional deep dugout	TW 21
	3rd		As on 2nd. Ordered to construct Heavy T.M. Emplacement in QUARRY	TW 21
	4th		As on 3rd. Started clearing way to proposed Heavy TM Emplacement	TW 21
	5th		As on 4th	TW 21
	6th		As on 5th had even stop work on H.T.M. Emplacement	TW 21
	7th		Ordered to hand over position for H.T.M. in TRAVERS KEEP.	
	8th		Reconnoitring position of Right Subsector MAROC and take	
			Ordered to gun up dubouts LOOS. blown up in JERMYN STREET	TW 21
			over one T.M. Emplacement blown up in JERMYN STREET	
			Medium T.M. Emplacement to one deep dugout	
			blocking entrances to SEVENTH AVENUE completed	
			Res SAA Store. No 1 Section (hint. Camp) proceeds to LOOS and	
	9th		As before. No 1 Section (hint. Camp) proceeds to LOOS and goes into billets there	TW 21

WAR DIARY or INTELLIGENCE SUMMARY

Army Form C. 2118

Place	Date	Hour	Summary of Events and Information	Remarks and references to Appendices
LES BREBIS	10th	—	Right Subsector handed over to 154th Field Coy RE. 37th Divn.	
do	11th	—	O.C. goes round new Left Subsector with O.C. 229 Field Coy RE. Arrangements made for distribution of working parties as eight can assume as eighth can assume	TM
do	12th	—	Taking over of Left Subsector completed. Work in hand Right Subsector – Three deep dugouts under construction (two finished this day). General trench maintenance. Left Subsector. One Medium T.M. Emplacement (under supervision of 229 Field Coy RE) Two Stokes T.M. Emplacements. Clearing of trenches: erection of trench shelters.	
do	13th	—	Work started on Heavy T.M. Emplacement TRAVERS KEEP. Ordered to start work on dugouts to suit normal location of Brigade – any two in MIDDLE ALLEY	
do	14th	—	in RESERVE Line. Medium T.M. Emplacement as before, making work on QUEEN ST.	

WAR DIARY or INTELLIGENCE SUMMARY

Army Form C. 2118

(Erase heading not required.)

Instructions regarding War Diaries and Intelligence Summaries are contained in F.S. Regs., Part II. and the Staff Manual respectively. Title Pages will be prepared in manuscript.

Place	Date	Hour	Summary of Events and Information	Remarks and references to Appendices
LES BREBIS	15th		No 2 Section (2nd Lt Clark) moving to LOOS	TWM
	16th		Work as before DOUBLE CRASSIER	
	17th		CRE made no work. Heavy bombardment of 110th Bde sector. Special damage done to: SOUTHERN CRASSIER, CRASSIER TRENCH, ST JAMES ST, BOYAU 30 and 32, REGENT ST and front line, BOYAU 39: HARTS and HARRISONS CRATERS all parties up trenches	TWM
	18th		O.C. 18th R.W.F. expresses his appreciation of good work done by No 1 + 2 Sections and their officers. Still engaged clearing up + making saps + unused trenches. Very wet day causing earth slips in trenches arrived before Brig Gen County becoming Bde (Lt Col Jones RE)	TWM TWM TWM TWM
	19th 20th 21st 22nd 23rd 24th		Work as before	TWM
	25th		Two officers 129th Infantry Fld Coy RE came to take over from Quinn killed by rifle grenade	TWM

1875. Wt. W593/826 1,000,000 4/15 J.B.C. & A. A.D.S.S./Forms/C.2118.

WAR DIARY
or
INTELLIGENCE SUMMARY

Army Form C. 2118

(Erase heading not required.)

Place	Date	Hour	Summary of Events and Information	Remarks and references to Appendices
LES BREBIS	26th		Work as before the HILLS	TWM
do	27th		Work as before. Raid attempted by three of MINENWERFER. Two lifters went out to complete the Bangalore torpedo in left subsector. Torpedo was not placed in wire owing to rifle & pistol fire - O.C. 129th Field Coy RE comes down to settle little details	TWM
do	28th		Two sections from LOOS rejoin their company	TWM
do	29th		129 Field Coy ammo and guns to GRENAY hills	TWM
do	30th		224 Field Coy moves to billets in LES BREBIS	TWM
do	30th		hunt ambulance & 12 men & 3 forward to BRUAY.	
do	30th		Coy - strength 7 offrs, 198 OR - march from LES BREBIS to BRUAY, leaving at 9.15 am arriving at 1.45 pm. Delayed owing to Carlisle Post not having received orders to have column. Three sections by infantry, one attached to HQS road occupied by infantry on road ordered to keep control, post on starting otherwise from distance. Heavy shower 11 miles	TWM

W. Mills
Capture
O C 224 Field Coy RE

Vol 6

Confidential

WAR DIARY

224th Field Company R.E.

November, 1916

VOLUME VI

Secret

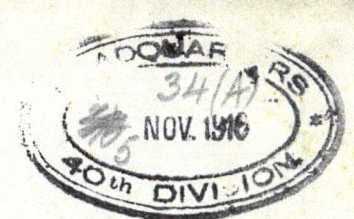

D.A.G.,
    3rd Echelon.

In continuation of this office minute No. 34(A) dated 3/11/16, herewith War Diary of 224th Field Company, R.E.

                                                                       fr Major-General,

5th November, 1916.   Commanding 40th Division.

WAR DIARY or INTELLIGENCE SUMMARY

Army Form C. 2118

Place	Date Nov	Hour	Summary of Events and Information	Remarks and references to Appendices
On the March	1st		Left BRUAY 8.30 am marching independently to HERLIN-LE-VERT. Arrived 1 pm. Weather fine. Billets poor. Distance 10 miles. Took horses off road owing to its being shown as good on map with road.	TWM
do.	2nd		Left HERLIN-LE-VERT at 8.30 am, marched to Right Column 121 Inf. Bde to near WAHAGNIES. Weather wet to start with improving later. Many ways through rather cramped. Distance 12 miles. Billets fair. No 1 Section RE had heavy wagon cemetery hole which descended a hill, a temporary while descending a hill, enabling holes to be brought in crack made with pick hides. No wait billet. Verbal orders received about 8 pm for move next day.	TWM
do.	3rd		Detailed orders for move only received at 7 am. Start made about 8.30 am. Marched behind 21st Inf. Bde to NEUVILLETTE. Distance 7 miles. Billets good. Limber wagons repaired by Former Sergeant and by wheeler.	

WAR DIARY or INTELLIGENCE SUMMARY

Army Form C. 2118

Place	Date	Hour	Summary of Events and Information	Remarks and references to Appendices
	4th		Resting at NEUVILLETTE. Orders received in AM for move next day to CANDAS. In P.M. verbal instructions received from B.G. Eng. 121 Inf Bde for move to COIGNEUX. Detailed orders received about 5 p.m.	WM
	5th		March to COIGNEUX via DOULLENS. Distance 15 miles, reporting to C.E. VIII Corps at COUIN. Afternoon spent in pitching tents, preparing cooking places, etc. Four Walker - Four	WM
	6th		O.C. reports to C.E. VIII Corps for instructions to send one section to BERTRAND COURT for erection of Corps Workshops. Remainder ordered to be employed on hutting camp.	
	7th		Company employed on hutting camp. Lt. Grantham with No 3 Section and one platoon moves to BERTRAND COURT. Remainder of company employed in and around wagon lines, moved no work possible owing to extremely almost no wood available for hutments for one battn on SALLE COIGNEUX- COURCELLES road	

Place	Date	Hour	Summary of Events and Information	Remarks and references to Appendices
	8th	—	No 1 Section employed in Camp. No 2 & 4 Sections levelling site for hutment camp. No 3 Section marking out site of Workshops. Weather — showery	App 4
	9th	—	As on 8th. Weather — bright but cold. No 3 Section commence erection of NISSEN Hut	App 5
	10th	—	No 2 & 4 Sections commence erection of NISSEN huts. No 1 Section marched out for a lecture from Capt. to COUIN to march out with instructions from SORE XIII Corps.	App 6
	11th	—	As on 10th. No 1 Section commence erection of Corps Work shops. No 3 Section commence erection of huts	App 7, App 8
	12th		As on before. Attack on German trenches by Huns as before.	App 9
	13th		Work as before. No 1, 2, and 4 Sections move out to huronia in huts.	
	14th		Work as before. No 1, 2, and 4 Sections move out to huts at THE DELL at COUIN in huts erected by them	App 9

WAR DIARY or INTELLIGENCE SUMMARY

Army Form C. 2118

(Erase heading not required.)

Place	Date	Hour	Summary of Events and Information	Remarks and references to Appendices
COIGNEUX	14th	—	Orders received from C.E. XIII Corps to place construction at disposal of B.G. Cmdg. 120th Inf Bde for work in the line. No 4 Section details with 2nd Lieut Pearson take over workshops and area occupied by 120th Inf Bde.	T.W.M.
do.	15th	—	H.Q.S. 120th Inf Bde arrive at COIGNEUX. O.C. and Lt Nicholson to see B.C. Cmdy. Other work as before.	T.W.M.
do.	16th	—	O.C. and Lt. Nicholson to HEBUTERNE. Other work as before. Two reports working parties report to assist in erecting hut camp at BAYEN-COURT. Ordered by C.E to take charge of BAYEN-COURT Camp.	T.W.M.
do	17th	.	Three sections continued work on huts and repair on loops workshop. Can at BAYENCOURT taken over by bay.	
do	18th	.	Work as before. Pumping station on HEBERTURNE	

WAR DIARY
or
INTELLIGENCE SUMMARY
(Erase heading not required.)

Army Form C. 2118

Place	Date	Hour	Summary of Events and Information	Remarks and references to Appendices
	1916 Nov 18	—	Taken over by day.	
	" 19		Work as before	
	" 20		do	
	" 21		Company proceeded to camp at COISNEUX. O.C. Company admitted to hospital at COUIN sick. Company marching to HEM independently under orders of 13th Corps. — 40th Division concentrated in DOULLENS area.	
	" 22			
	" 23		1 Company marched independently to BERTEAUCOURT under Orders No. 105/30. St Elmers proceeded to England on leave.	
	" 24		1 Company left BERTEAUCOURT in column of Route in company with 12th Suffolks, 13th East Lancs, 14th Argyll & Sutherlands. 2nd Lt Machine took over command. 4th Divisional train and 13th Infantry Headquarters to PONT REMY.	
	" 25		Rest & Refresh up.	
	" 26		Company moved independently to L'ETOILE. Lt Col Belmont & 2 Lt Nicholson proceeded on leave to England.	

Army Form C. 2118

WAR DIARY
or
INTELLIGENCE SUMMARY
(Erase heading not required.)

Place	Date	Hour	Summary of Events and Information	Remarks and references to Appendices
	1916 Nov 27		All his Equipment checked and overhauled. Deficiencies noted.	
	" 28		Continuation of Kit and Equipment cleaning. Arrangements made for opening of Brigade Workshop for improvements in Bridge Moulding Purpose area.	
	" 29		Inspection of Company's equipment by D.A.D.S. Issue of Bar Rapiators to Company under supervision of Divisional Gas School. Two lorry loads of timber received from C.R.E. for Bridge improvements. Gave orders once and Physical Exercises were supervised by Section Officers.	
	" 30.		Continuation of Class Order Drill & Physical Training under Section Officers. Two Pontoon loads of stores drawn from HANOEST for R.E. 40th Division for Bridge improvements and training purposes throughout Divisional area.	

Army Form C. 2118

WAR DIARY
or
INTELLIGENCE SUMMARY
(Erase heading not required.)

Place	Date	Hour	Summary of Events and Information	Remarks and references to Appendices
	Nov 30		One Officer appointed Town Major of the L'ETOILE — D.A.I. to kept. One Officer appointed on Board of Enquiry, per 40th Division order No. 809 of Nov. 29/1916.	

E.M.Smith Lt Col R.E.
Comdg 234 Field Coy R.E.
Nov. 30/1916

Confidential

War Diary
of
224th Field Coy R.E.

December, 1916.   Volume VII

Army Form C. 2118

WAR DIARY
or
INTELLIGENCE SUMMARY

(Erase heading not required.)

December 1916   224th Field Coy. R.E., H.Q. Division

Instructions regarding War Diaries and Intelligence Summaries are contained in F.S. Regs., Part II. and the Staff Manual respectively. Title Pages will be prepared in manuscript.

Place	Date	Hour	Summary of Events and Information	Remarks and references to Appendices
ETOILE	1st		In Rest. Drill. Improvement of billets. Orders received to move into forward area.	TWM
	2nd		ditto.	TWM
	3rd to 7th		ditto. Lieut. E.M. Smith to H.Q. 4th Army to take over Jeanville lines. ditto.	TM
	8th		Coy Transport left L'ETOILE and marched to ARQUEVES together with transport of 9in. Pioneers, 229 and 231 Field Coys. Capt MILLER rejoins from Hospital in evening.	TWM
	9th		Coy paraded at 2.30 am and marches 7 miles to PONT REMY, entraining about 7.30 am under orders of O.C. 12th Yorks R (Pioneers). Detrain about 1 pm at MERICOURT to march 8 miles to BRAY arriving about 5 pm. Billets taken over in the dark. March very slow owing to congested state of roads. Men very tired. Transport also moved to BRAY arriving about 7 pm: no limes, vehicles parked by roadside, horses tied	

WAR DIARY or INTELLIGENCE SUMMARY

Army Form C. 2118

(2)

Place	Date	Hour	Summary of Events and Information	Remarks and references to Appendices
	10		to vehicles	
			Paraded 8.20am marching to MAVRE PAS CAMP 12km. Transport blocked by French columns moving West and fails to catch up dismounted party. As a result men have to carry packs 9 extra 5 miles. No accommodation available before 5pm. Then a few very poor shelters for officers and to tents for men are all that is provided. Only slight rain but ground sodden and extremely filthy owing to previous occupation by French troops. Company only just settled in before it was too dark to work. Men marched extremely well but very tired. No accommodation for horses or vehicles.	TW M
AGREPAS	11		Rations for consumption on this day not received until 8 pm owing to no supplying part having been notified. Men ordered to eat iron rations. Transport lines established	TWM

1875 Wt. W593/826 1,000,000 4/15 J.B.C. & A. A.D.S.S./Forms/C. 2118.

(3)

Army Form C. 2118

WAR DIARY
or
INTELLIGENCE SUMMARY
(Erase heading not required.)

Place	Date	Hour	Summary of Events and Information	Remarks and references to Appendices
MAUREPAS	12th		Improving Camp	
do	13th		O.C. 229 Fd. Coy goes round with B.G.G.S. and C.E. XV Corps. reconnoitring positions of strong points in intermediate line.	
do	14th		Coy improving Camp. O.C. goes along intermediate line with O.C. 229 Field Coy R.E.	
do	15th		Work commenced on trenches from which to make dug outs for machine gunners. No.1 Section working at night. No.2 Section is heavily shelled when starting to start work: decided to work there also at first.	
do	16th		Continuing work. Lieut. HEAVISIDES arrives to replace Lieut SMITH.	
do	17th		As before. 4 reinforcements (2 drivers 2 sappers) arrive.	
do	18th		As before. 2 sections start working on dugouts.	

(4)

Army Form C. 2118

Instructions regarding War Diaries and Intelligence Summaries are contained in F.S. Regs., Part II. and the Staff Manual respectively. Title Pages will be prepared in manuscript.

WAR DIARY
or
INTELLIGENCE SUMMARY
(Erase heading not required.)

Place	Date	Hour	Summary of Events and Information	Remarks and references to Appendices
MAUREPAS	19th		Corps machine gun officer goes along line. Three sites approved and lines of fire settled. Decided to move positions of 3 & 4 MG's further north	TM 2
do.	20th		Work continued on dugouts. Work continued on dugouts. Jungle line of wire thoroughfare commenced.	TM 2
do	21st		As on 20th.	TM 4
do	22nd		Work as on 20th. Wiring of jungle line partially completed with O.C. 222 Field Coy R.E. to take over O.C. round with Right of Bde Sector of 91nd Front	TM 2
do	23rd 24th 25th		Work as on 20th. Parties from N° 3 Section sent forward to take over billets from 222 Field Coy R.E.; also from N° 1 Section to take over billets from 11th Field Coy. Remainder resting	TM 4

WAR DIARY or INTELLIGENCE SUMMARY

Army Form C. 2118

Place	Date	Hour	Summary of Events and Information	Remarks and references to Appendices
LE FOREST	26th		Move. No 1 Section moves to DOMINO DUMP to take over billets there until arrival of 231 Field Coy R.E. No 2, 3, and 4 Sections and Headquarters to LE FOREST: Transport to MAUREPAS. Occupied in settling in.	TW 2
do	27th		Decided that it is impossible to continue work on existing Battn Headquarters, and that it is unwise to make a fresh start. No 1 Section at work at DOMINO DUMP: No 3 on dugout for Advanced Field Coy billets: No 2 on Battn HQ dugouts: No 4 work in Camp.	TW 3
do	28th		Work as on 27th: also 5″O Infantry at work on ABBOT LANE. No 1 Section relieved by 231 Field Coy R.E. and moves to LE FOREST.	TW 4
do	29th		ABODE LANE: 5″O Infantry at work on ABODE LANE. As on 28th: new trench to replace ABODE LANE decided to dig rather than open up existing trench. Sites selected by BCle for temporary Gun & Boot Stores and Bomb Store.	TW 5

WAR DIARY

INTELLIGENCE SUMMARY

Army Form C. 2118

Place	Date	Hour	Summary of Events and Information	Remarks and references to Appendices
LE FOREST	30th		Work as before. No 3 starts work on Gun Boot Store and Bomb Store. Communication Trench 100 Infantry on each.	TW_M
do.	31st		Work as on 30th, but no night parties, owing to Battn Relief.	TW_M

W. Muller
Major RE
O.C. 224 Fld Coy RE

Confidential

Vol 8

War Diary
of
224th Field Company RE

month of January 1917

VOLUME VIII

Army Form C. 2118

WAR DIARY
INTELLIGENCE SUMMARY
(Erase heading not required.)

January

Place	Date	Hour	Summary of Events and Information	Remarks and references to Appendices
LE FOREST	Jan 1st	—	Work continued as before viz Day work on communication Trenches Dugout for Battn. Headquarters, construction of Temporary Bde Dressing Room and Gun Boot Store, Bde Bomb Store, R.E. advanced Wrkshts. No night parties available owing to Battn. relief.	TWM
	2nd	—	O.C. 1st Home Counties Coy R.E. (T.F.) came to arrange taking over of our sector. Lt. Grantham goes round M.G. positions with O.C. 119th Machine Gun Coy. O.C. goes round with O.C. 1st H.C. Coy R.E. (T.F.). Work continued as on 1st; also night party on ABODE C.T. Working parties all very short. Machine Gun Coy at work on shelters for gun teams near selected positions.	TWM
	3rd	—	As on 2nd. with in addition work on ATLAS TRENCH and commencement of a dugout for Lewis Machine Guns in	TWM
HOSPITAL WOOD.	4th	—	Little work done owing to relief of 119th Inf Bde by 120th Inf Bde. R.E Work as on previous days.	TWM

Army Form C. 2118

WAR DIARY
or
INTELLIGENCE SUMMARY
(Erase heading not required.)

Instructions regarding War Diaries and Intelligence Summaries are contained in F.S. Regs., Part II. and the Staff Manual respectively. Title Pages will be prepared in manuscript.

January

Place	Date	Hour	Summary of Events and Information	Remarks and references to Appendices
	5th	—	Working parties start well. Deviation to ABODE LANE cleared day to 3 feet deep for 120ˣ. Other work as before.	TW 24
	6th	—	Working as before. Trench dug on 5.1.16 deepened to 5 feet for 100ˣ. ANDES (ABBOT) LANE cleared up to Right Battn HQS	TW 14
	7th	—	Working as before. ABODE LANE extended for 60ˣ depth 2'6". 50ˣ cleared and trenchboarded, 50ˣ partially cleared	TW 2
	8th	—	No infantry parties available owing to Battn reliefs. R.E. continued work as before.	TW 2
	9th	—	Work as before. Continued clearing ABODE LANE, but work very heavy on account of rain having caused many falls and in places flooded trench.	TW 21

1875 Wt. W593/826 1,000,000 4/15 J.B.C. & A. A.D.S.S./Forms/C. 2118.

WAR DIARY
or
INTELLIGENCE SUMMARY
(Erase heading not required.)

Army Form C. 2118

Instructions regarding War Diaries and Intelligence Summaries are contained in F. S. Regs., Part II. and the Staff Manual respectively. Title Pages. will be prepared in manuscript.

Place	Date	Hour	Summary of Events and Information	Remarks and references to Appendices
LE FOREST	10th	—	Work as before. Temporary Gun Boat Store completed. Gang party clearing out newetting ANDES Trench. myhle party clearing and trenchering portion of ABODE LANE already dug	
do	11th	—		TW 4/1
do	12th	—	Work as on 10th. ABODE LANE advanced about 50'. One chamber of Bde Bomb Store completed. Work started on Regt. aid Post for Left Battn. Only working parties available were day party improving accommodation at APOLLO, and night party to heavy hostile letter party did not work owing to shelling. 120th Inf Bde relieved by 121 Inf Bde.	TW 4
do	13th	—	the Trenshill slightly wounded whilst working at A 215" Work continued as before. Chambering commenced on left Battn H⁄Q 43847 for Left Cookh and 51762 Lft & twn.	TW 4/2 TW 4/3 TW 4/4
do	14th	—	Work continued as before. Well actually just outside stable bulkhg 43847. For Left cook hs(?) 18069 the Register (sighted) at ABODE LANE, chamng and firing to agron started down to depths. shelters	TW 4
do	15th	—	newetting Right Battn H Q S down completed for 120 men & different Battns	TW 4

WAR DIARY or INTELLIGENCE SUMMARY

Army Form C. 2118

(Erase heading not required.)

Instructions regarding War Diaries and Intelligence Summaries are contained in F.S. Regs., Part II. and the Staff Manual respectively. Title Pages will be prepared in manuscript.

Place	Date	Hour	Summary of Events and Information	Remarks and references to Appendices
LE FOREST	16th		Dug outs put in firm trench almost in ABODE LANE. at night, this party was taken over by the remainder of infantry under Capt. KIRBY, 13th E. Yorks R. Other work continued as before.	TW 2/
do	17th		Work continued as before, clearing and revetting ANDES LANE and ABODE LANE. RE already billets. Bde Bomb stores, and Lewis gun dugouts constructions of shelters for support Battn and for Regt. and Post. Permanent party at work at night on ABODE LANE	TW 4
do	18th		Work as before. Permanent party revetting in ABODE LANE Started work extending and clearing equally Right Battn dugout; and started improving condition of Reserve Company's Right Battn	TW H TW 2
do	19th		Work as before. Heavy fall of work in Left Battn dugout; one now being caught but being extended practically whole. Work started on clearing dugout in sunken road near ABODE LANE	TW 2

WAR DIARY
INTELLIGENCE SUMMARY
(Erase heading not required.)

Army Form C. 2118

January

Place	Date	Hour	Summary of Events and Information	Remarks and references to Appendices
LE FOREST	20th		Work as before. Work started on ANDES LANE East of BETHUNE ROAD.	TW/23
do	21st		Work as before ABODE LANE trenchboarded as far as sunken road. Sergt A COOPER No 99215- killed by shell fire on Q walk.	TW 24
do	22nd		Work as before 121 Inf Bde relieved by 119 Inf Bde	TW 26
do	23rd		Work as before, but progress on Right Battn HQS and Support Battn shelters much reduced by lack of working parties.	TW 27
do	24th		Work as before. Box Body Mine completed. Regt. Aid Post APOLLO completed. No work on Right Battn HQS and Support Battn shelters. Warned to be prepared to hand over on 26th inst and move on 27th inst. Lepr Wilkinson No 1 sect wounded on shelterwork near A 215.	TW 28 TW 29
do	25th		Work as before.	
do	26th		No work after 7am. Company concentrating and preparing to move. Officer of Home Counties RE, 6th Q <?> comes to take over	TW 31

Army Form C. 2118

WAR DIARY
or
INTELLIGENCE SUMMARY
(Erase heading not required.)

January

Place	Date	Hour	Summary of Events and Information	Remarks and references to Appendices
LE FOREST	27th		Company paraded at 8.30 am and marched by sections to Camp 14: distance 14 miles. Roads good. Weather very fair. Camp poor. Weather very cold.	TW 4
do.	28th		Easy day. Weather intensely cold. O.C. 224 C.R.E. copy of Troops and gets instructions as to work: re demolition of Camp 14 and reception at new site.	TW 5
do.	29th		Work started: three huts pulled down. New site marked out. Pontoons fitched from MAUREPAS.	TW 6
do.	30th		Work continued. Now hut demolished. One carted to rear.	
do.	31st		Work continued. Three motor lorries obtained for carting huts to new site. MILLER goes to Engineering course LE PARCQ.	TW 7

TW Miller
Major R.E.
O.C. 224 Field Coy R.E.

CONFIDENTIAL

224th Inf Bgy
29 of 9

A.F. 2118. WAR DIARY February 1917

Vol 9

WAR DIARY
or
INTELLIGENCE SUMMARY
(Erase heading not required.)

Army Form C. 2118

February 1917.

Place	Date	Hour	Summary of Events and Information	Remarks and references to Appendices
Camp 14.	Feb 1st		3 huts taken down & stacked, huts for 1 hut taken to new site. 1 large latrine taken down & carted to road.	
do.	" 2nd		Up to end of today, 13 huts taken down, stacked & carted to new site. 1 hut almost completed on new site. Drains for 5 huts dug on new site.	
do.	" 3rd		Up to end of today 17 huts have been removed from old site & carted away to new site. One hut being erected at new site.	
do.	" 4th		General overhauling of rifles, kit, etc. Church service in the afternoon by Rev. Bellman.	
do.	" 5th		Continued removing huts from old site & constructing same on new site.	

WAR DIARY or INTELLIGENCE SUMMARY

Army Form C. 2118

February 1917

Place	Date	Hour	Summary of Events and Information	Remarks and references to Appendices
Camp 14.	6th		Continued removal of huts to Neuville. Had assistance of 125 Infantry. One complete hut taken to Harcourt for erection there.	
do	7th		Continued removal of huts. Up to end of today 11 huts have been removed to new site, 3 being erected complete & 5 in progress. Tool Carts cleaned & painted.	
do	8th		Removal of huts from Camp 14 & erection of same on new site in progress.	
do	9th		Up to end of this day 15 large huts have been taken down & 14 taken from old site. 12 huts are under construction at new site of these 6 are completed. Severe frost prevents any drainage scheme being carried out.	
do	10th		Continued removal of huts. Lt Grantham goes on course of instruction, to school of instruction (Infantry) 4th Army. 2/Lt Clark Church service in the afternoon.	
do	11th		Removal of huts. Proceeded to Sailly-le-Sec to work under CRE XV Corps Troops. & Section 2.	

WAR DIARY
INTELLIGENCE SUMMARY
(Erase heading not required.)

Army Form C. 2118

Instructions regarding War Diaries and Intelligence Summaries are contained in F.S. Regs., Part II. and the Staff Manual respectively. Title Pages will be prepared in manuscript. **February 1917.**

Place	Date	Hour	Summary of Events and Information	Remarks and references to Appendices
Camp 14.	Feb. 12th		Continued removal of huts. One hut erected from old site to MARICOURT & completed, for use of R.A.M.C.	
do.	13th		Continued removal of huts. Capt C.M. Smith rejoins Company from leave to England.	
do.	14th		Removal of huts continued. Frost still holds out.	
do.	15th		Continued removal of huts. Change of weather, thaw sets in + a little rainfall.	
do.	16th		Up to end of today 22 large huts taken down & 21½ taken away to new site. 2 Officers' huts taken to new site & one erected.	
do.	17th		Continued removal of huts.	
do.	18th		Owing to receipt of telegram (adopt thaw precautions) no transport available. Dismantling huts on old site & erection of huts on new site continued.	
do.	19th		No transport available, but work continued on both sites	

Army Form C. 2118.

WAR DIARY
INTELLIGENCE SUMMARY
(Erase heading not required.)

February 1919

Place	Date	Hour	Summary of Events and Information	Remarks and references to Appendices
Camp 14	Feb 20th		No transport available, work continued at both sites. Owing to thaw & rain, the ground at new site becomes very soft & wet.	
do	21st		Work carried on at new site, erection & a little drainage carried on.	
do	22nd		No transport available, work carried on at new site. 110 Notice Boards painted & forwarded to SAILLY-LE-SEC.	
do	23rd		Up to end of today 23 large huts have been dismantled, 21½ taken to new site. 18 large huts completed on new site & 1 half completed. 2 officers huts completed & Camp Commandants office erected. A little work done on drainage. Ground just underneath surface still very hard.	
do	24th		No transport available, carried on with drainage & general repair to huts damaged in transit.	
do	25th		Draining continued on new site. No transport available owing to thaw precautions.	

WAR DIARY or INTELLIGENCE SUMMARY.

Army Form C. 2118.

February

Place	Date	Hour	Summary of Events and Information	Remarks and references to Appendices
Camp 14	26th		Major MILLER returns from course. One section at work on new site. Two sections doing nothing, training.	W.4
do.	27th		do. on 26th. Wanted to move to new position.	W.4
do.	28th		Wanted to go into line at CLERY. Arranged to go in to Prisoners Camp near new Camp 14. Three sections preparing for move.	W.4

T W Milly
Major R.E.
O.C. 224 Field Coy R.E.

War Diary

226th Field Coy R.E.

From 1st March 1917

To 31st March 1917

Volume 10

WAR DIARY
INTELLIGENCE SUMMARY

224th Field Co. R.E.

March 1917

Army Form C. 2118.

Place	Date	Hour	Summary of Events and Information	Remarks and references to Appendices
Camp 14 (old site)	1st		O.C. goes up to CLERY to arrange preliminaries as to taking over. Capt Smith wants new horse lines. 2 Lt Nicholson & No 4 Section proceed to PRISONERS CAMP near BRAY.	TW M
	2nd		O.C. goes to new sector to take over work. Company less No 2 and 4 Sections move to PRISONERS CAMP.	TW M
do	3rd		O.C. returns to Company. 2 Lt Clark and No 2 Section rejoin from SAILLY-LE-SEC.	TW M
do	4th		Men bathing. Officers demolition scheme.	TW M

WAR DIARY
or
INTELLIGENCE SUMMARY.
(Erase heading not required.)

Army Form C. 2118.

Place	Date	Hour	Summary of Events and Information	Remarks and references to Appendices
Proven Camp	5th	—	Men drilling etc. NCO's demolition scheme. Preparing for move.	TW/y
Camp 161	6th	—	Whole company move by water to Camp 161, wanted to CLERY to reserve owing to some trouble in other units moving by 23th Field Coy R.E. Lieut. Clark + advanced party moved to CLERY to take over billets. Advanced party to horse lines at FRISE BEND.	TW/y
CLERY	7th	—	Dismounted portion of company moved to dugouts off WURZEL AVENUE. Mounted portion to horse lines and dugouts at FRISE BEND. Under Capt. Smith.	TW/y

WAR DIARY
INTELLIGENCE SUMMARY.

Army Form C. 2118.

Month: March 1917

Place	Date	Hour	Summary of Events and Information	Remarks and references to Appendices
CLERY	8-		Officers reconnaissance. Improvement of shelter. 113 Inf Bde HQS moved in in enemy	App IV
do.	9-		Scheme of work submitted to Brigade. NCOs reconnaissance. Improvement of RE huts. Support Battn ends relieves in enemy. Scheme of work has to be considerably altered owing to Pwd. Pioneers having altogether stopped work in MAUD AVENUE, without reference to Bde HQ	two
do	10-		Work started. No 1 Section on 3 machine gun dugouts. No 2 Section work on Bde HQS and RE huts (shelters - 3 completed and cookhouse shelter, water supply improved) N° 3 Section working in Right Battn Area (considerable work on T.M.E.'s & FRECKLES LANE cleaned)	two

Army Form C. 2118.

WAR DIARY
or
INTELLIGENCE SUMMARY.
(Erase heading not required.)

Place	Date	Hour	Summary of Events and Information	Remarks and references to Appendices
CLERY	11th		Work continued as on 10th	TWM
do	12th		Work continued as on 11th	TWM
do	13th		Work continued as on 12th. No 2 section started clearing cellars in CLERY to form bomb stores. Very little work done owing to absence of infantry parties. Wind NW every to	TWM
do	14		Work continued. Wind same as noted.	TWM
do	15th		Work continued as before. Wind NW every to 2hr. Brigade relief.	
do	16th		Wind N veering to NE and backing to N. Little work owing to no Infantry parties. 2 Lieut WYNTER NICHOLSON wounded by shrapnel outside officers billets CLERY; died an advanced dressing station two hours later.	
do	17th		Work continued. 9 Infantry occupied German front line in afternoon and evening	TWM

Army Form C. 2118.

WAR DIARY
or
INTELLIGENCE SUMMARY.

(Erase heading not required.)

Place	Date	Hour	Summary of Events and Information	Remarks and references to Appendices
CLERY	17 contd		Pte HEAVISIDES and CLARK assist infantry consolidation. Two Sappers go out with infantry patrol and bring back valuable report on CLERY-PERONNE main Road.	TWM
CLERY	18th		2/Lt CLARK goes out with infantry patrol and is the first man into MONT ST QUENTIN. Furnishes valuable report on bridges and roads in the vicinity of FEAVILLE COURT. Carpentry R.E. assisting Infantry in consolidating new line of resistance and forward post at MONT ST. QUENTIN. Repair of bridge over SOMME between CLERY and O MIE COURT.	TWM

Place	Date	Hour	Summary of Events and Information	Remarks and references to Appendices
CLERY	18th	-	Bridge over TORTILLE River CLERY – PERONNE Road started. Lieut CARR reconnoitres River SOMME between CLERY and PERONNE for proposed bridges.	WD
do	19th	-	New line of resistance established from HILL 75 to MONT ST QUENTIN. Two sections working. Completion of two bridges worked on on 18th. Another bridge over River TORTILLE completed in FEVILLECOURT. Party repairing roads	WD

Army Form C. 2118.

WAR DIARY
or
INTELLIGENCE SUMMARY.
(Erase heading not required.)

Instructions regarding War Diaries and Intelligence Summaries are contained in F. S. Regs., Part II. and the Staff Manual respectively. Title pages will be prepared in manuscript.

Place	Date	Hour	Summary of Events and Information	Remarks and references to Appendices
LERY	20th		Two sections helping Infantry in line Lt. HEAVISIDES reconnoitring MONT ST QUENTIN for billets	TWM
	21		Lieut Clark and No 2 Section moved forward into Billets at the Cemetery at LE QUINCONEE	
	22		3 Section moved forward with Infantry - 1 Section being employed on Strong point at RED HOUSE, work out post East	
	23		2 Section employed on consolidation employment work East holding line of roadways East of BUSSU. Section & Stores along moved to LE QUINCONEE HEAD QUARTERS above. Continued work Infantry. MAJOR MILLER admitted to Hospital	
	24		Continued work in advanced area and No 2 Section moved into Billets at OMMIECOURT to prepare BDE H. QRS	

WAR DIARY
or
INTELLIGENCE SUMMARY.

Army Form C. 2118.

Place	Date	Hour	Summary of Events and Information	Remarks and references to Appendices
CLERY	25		Nos 3 and 4 Section marched from BUSSU to the new H.Qrs Billets at P.C. WURZEL. No 2 Section continued work at Cable house at H.Qrs. No 1 Section another eight hours on Mont St Quentin. Returning afterwards. Also No Infantry Company from P.C. WURZEL moving into Billets at P.C. WURZEL. HEAD QUARTERS. Horse Lines also moved up to P.C. WURZEL. Received from Base 4 Reinforcements. Whole Company employed on shelving & grooming and attending to Horses.	
	26		CLERY. FEUILLAUCOURT. HAUT-ALLAINS and MOISLAINS. DIVISIONAL Arrangements. Infantry Garrison for Posts. Received from Base Reinforcements about for this work. Received 4 Sappers. Horses & 1 Sapper.	
	27		Continues work as above. portion of men CLERY. FEUILLAUCOURT BRIDE Anlage complete & ready to hand on for transportation. Ross marched for Horse Lines out to MOISLAINS. Received Reinforcements from Base. 4 Sappers & 1 spare. marched to Wingfield Arrive	

WAR DIARY
or
INTELLIGENCE SUMMARY.

Army Form C. 2118.

Place	Date	Hour	Summary of Events and Information	Remarks and references to Appendices
CLERY	28		Coy. continued as before. Road open to MOISLAINS. 1 man admitted to Hospital	all troops
"	29		Work continued on road as before. No 3 Section with one battalion working on road MOISLAINS – NURLU. Received from Base reinforcement Camp – 2 sappers.	
"	30.		Work continued on road as above.	
"	31.		Work continued on roads. No 4 Section + one battalion transferred to MOISLAINS – NURLU road. Capt H. R. R. Gough attached to Company.	

E White Captain
for O.C. 224 Field Coy R.E.

31.3.17.

CONFIDENTIAL

WAR DIARY

Vol. XI

224th (FIELD) COMPANY R.E.

April. 1917.

WAR DIARY
or
INTELLIGENCE SUMMARY

April 1917

Army Form C. 2118.

Place	Date	Hour	Summary of Events and Information	Remarks and references to Appendices
Clery	1st		Strength of Coy. 6 Officers 191 O.R.	
			Attached 2 " 4 "	
			Hospital 1 " 8 "	
			No. One Section with one battalion clearing & sweeping HAUT-ALLAINES – MOISLAINS Road.	
			No. One Section with one battalion clearing & sweeping MOISLAINS – NURLU Road.	
			No. 3 & 4 Section two battalion Infty. clearing & repairing	
			Above three sections & Infantry worked 8 hours on road, 3 were away from CAMP 12 hours.	
			No. 2 Section rebuilding bridge over TORTILLE. Decking of wheels had been broken by badly driven lorry. 5" either road beaver was added making total beam average diameter of road –	map ref. bridge I.9.a.3.1.
			10"x10", span 16'. Bridge now considered safe up to 14 tons, extra carts abuts were also added. Bridge to decked ★ 4"x 3" timbers. 20 men employed for 8 hours. To hospital. 2 O.R.	
do	2nd		No. 3 & 4 section continued work on above.	
			No. 1 Section with one battalion clearing, draining & removing fallen trees from ST DENIS – AIZECOURT Road.	
			No. 2 Section ten men, sheeting & deepening water way of above bridge over TORTILLE	
			Map ref. I.9.a.3.1.	

WAR DIARY
or
INTELLIGENCE SUMMARY

Army Form C. 2118.

April 1917

Place	Date	Hour	Summary of Events and Information	Remarks and references to Appendices
Moisy	3rd		No 1 Section continued work with one Battalion on ST DENIS. — AIZECOURT Road.	
			" 2 " " " " " " " "	
			" " " " " HAUT-ALLAINS. — MOISLAINS Road worked to haven	
			No 3 & 4 section in CAMP. inspected & instructed by Section Officers in Arms & Gas drill. Clothing & equipment.	
			1 OR returned to Coy from 239 A.T. Coy.	
do	4th		No 4 section with one Battalion of Infantry worked on ST DENIS. — AIZECOURT Road	
			cleaning, sweeping, on face on each side. D. & d. o. 4.	
			No 3 Section removing twigs over WURZEL TRENCH, H.5.c.9.3. & filling & making	
			up road. 20 sappers employed 7 hours.	
			No 1 & 2 Section in CAMP. inspected & instructed by Section Officers in Arms & Gas drill.	
			Clothing & equipment.	
			2 O.R. joint Coy from N° 3 Reinforcement to R.E.	
do	5th		Sections 1 & 2 moved to FINS. Prepare Billets & accommodation for	
			Brigade Headquarters.	
			No. 3. Section completed work at on filling in crating WURZEL	
			TRENCH. H5c.9.3.	
			No. 4 Section continued work on AIZECOURT — NURLU Road.	

Army Form C. 2118.

WAR DIARY
or
INTELLIGENCE SUMMARY.
(Erase heading not required.)

APRIL 1917.

Place	Date	Hour	Summary of Events and Information	Remarks and references to Appendices
CUERN.	5th		Lt. Evans left Company on Special leave. Capt. Murphy returned to Divisional Headquarters.	
	6th		1 O.R. joined Coy. from No. 3. Reinforcement Coy. R.E. 1 O.R. & No. 3. Section moved to FINS. No. 4 Section moved to Headquarter Transport at dismounting OMMIÉCOURT.	
FINS.	7th		No. 4 Section moved to FINS. No. 1 & 2. Sections became Anti. R.E.A. group. Horse Lines & accommodation for Company & Brigade Headquarters. 2 – O.R.s Reformed temporary from leave. 1 N.C.O. & 10 men. 121 T.M.B. attached to Company for work on Dump. 1 O.R. to Hospital.	
FINS.	8th		No. 1. Section employed on 2 Strong points in 24th Battalion sector with 1 Company Infantry working party. No. 2. Section employed on Strong point in Regt' Battalion sector with 2 Platoons Infantry working party. No. 3. Section filling shell in FINS. left as large marks by unloading dump. 1 Section of Brigade Headquarters. 1. O.R. wounded by shrapnel whilst working on Strong Point.	Strength of Coy. Officers 7. O.R. 209. do. to 1. do. 3. Attached to 1. do. 8. Hospital

WAR DIARY or INTELLIGENCE SUMMARY

Army Form C. 2118.

(Erase heading not required.)

Place	Date	Hour	Summary of Events and Information	Remarks and references to Appendices
FINS.	9th		No.1 Section preparing & carrying out work & 2 Platoons of Infantry Q.33.c.2.7. & mining.	
			No.2 Section. Demolition of House at Q.35.c.5.0. N.A.a.b. Charges used for House Demolition 2 slabs	
			GOUZEACOURT Road. N.A.a.b. Charges used for House Demolition 2 slabs	
			& 1 fothmm. House destroyed receiving two gable ends.	
			No.2 Section. Hastily prepared & wired 2 machine gun positions in sunken	
			road Q.33.b.	
			No.3 Section. Road supervision FINS-EQUANCOURT. Holes sunken &	
			clearing in above places.	
			No.4 Section. Gates in GOUZEACOURT Road. W.3c.	
			Wire dump established at QUEEN'S CROSS.	
			No.1 Section. [text] with 1 Company Infantry put out	
			single line of wire from Northern Boundary to Q.27.b.2.4. (1200 yards).	
to	10th		No.2 Section. Put out wire from Q.23.d. extend through GOUZEACOURT WOOD	
			to point Q.27.b.7.3. (900 yards).	
			made good & continued filling craters on GOUZEACOURT Road &	
			made further attempts to demolish gable of House at N.A. [text] Q.35.c.5.0.	
			No.3 Section continued work on wells. Horse troughs, Roads & Signs.	
			2.O.R. admitted Hospital. 1 man 115 D.L.I. (Purpuses) attached for Rations	

A5834 Wt.W4973/M687 750,000 8/16 D.D. & L.Ltd. Forms/C.2118/13. 4/o A. Section continued work on Crater

WAR DIARY or INTELLIGENCE SUMMARY

Army Form C. 2118.

Place	Date	Hour	Summary of Events and Information	Remarks and references to Appendices
FINS.	11th		Nos. 1 & 2. Sections continued work as on the 10th.	
			No. 3. Section continued road work in EQUANCOURT and FINS.	
			No. 4. Section continued work on Baths.	
			1. O.R. Reinforcement.	
			7 men 119 Bn P.S. (Ionian) attached for Rations.	
do.	12th		No. 1. Section consolidated & worked strong point at Q.33.b.4.6.	
			No. 2. Section consolidated & wired strong point at QUEENS CROSS.	
			No. 3. Section continued work on Roads. Wells & Water Points commenced.	
			Drainage of craters in FINS.	
			No. 4. Section continued work on Craill. GOUZEAUCOURT Road.	
			1. O.R. Reinforcement.	
			7 men 119 Bn P.S. (Ionian) attached for Rations. 1 O.R. rejoined Unit from Hospital.	
do.	13th		No. 1 & 2. Sections continued demolition of houses in GOUZEAUCOURT Road &	
			and demolition of house at Q.35.c.8.0. Average Built of Mne. 2'9".	
			Charges used 8 slabs p/r hrs. Tunnel suffered in all cases but Mne.	
			effectly been felled.	
			No. 3. Section continued drainage of craters & road cleaning in FINS & EQUANCOURT.	

WAR DIARY
or
INTELLIGENCE SUMMARY.
(Erase heading not required.)

Army Form C. 2118.

April 1917

Place	Date	Hour	Summary of Events and Information	Remarks and references to Appendices
FINS.	13th contd.	—	Nos. 4 Section work on crates as before.	
		2.0 P.m.	Reinforcement. 1 O.R. admitted Hospital.	
	14th	—	Reconnaissance 1 Battalion Infantry commenced work on trench. Nos 1 & 2 Sections heavy & and new line of trenches is to commence in next night. No. 3 Section north continuation FINS to Nurlu roads & craters. No. 4 Section work on crates as before. No. 1 Section with 1 Battalion Infantry (350 strong) commenced work on new line as dug about 500 yards. No. 2 Section marked out line & continuous road clearing GOUZEAUCOURT road.	
	15th		Nos. 3 & 4 Sections work as before. 1 officer & 1 O.R. to Hospital.	
			Strength of Coy. Attached. Hospital.	Officers. 7. 1. 1. O.R.s 208. 21. 7.

A.5834 Wt.W4973/M687 750,000 8/16 D. D. & L. Ltd. Forms/C.2118/13.

WAR DIARY
or
INTELLIGENCE SUMMARY.

Army Form C. 2118.

April. 1917.

Place	Date	Hour	Summary of Events and Information	Remarks and references to Appendices
FINS.	16th	—	131st. Brigade Works Company. Officers nil. O.R. 157. attached to Company. Discipline. Rations. Accommodation & work. Employed on preparing Billets for themselves. No. 1 & 2 Sections. commenced wiring on Left Battalion front. No. 4. Section wiring Right Battalion front. Forward Dump established for Wire & Pickets available for this line. Line worked upon was to be a Divisional Main Line of Resistance, known as the Brown Line. No. 3. Section continued work in FINS. on Wells. Culverts. Horse Troughs. Signboards &c.	
do.	17th.		No. 1. Section with 2 Platoons. Works Company worked in daylight clearing & deepening trenches in GOUZEACOURT WOOD. 600 yards thereof completed. Northern edge of GOUZEACOURT WOOD. also completed. 400 yards wire completed. No. 2. Section & No. 4. Section continued wiring by night. Left Battalion front. Brown Line. 1 Platoon Works Coy. acted as carrying party. No. 3. Section continued work as before. Works Company completing Billets.	

WAR DIARY
INTELLIGENCE SUMMARY

APRIL 1917

Place	Date	Hour	Summary of Events and Information	Remarks and references to Appendices
FINS.	17th contd.		Lt. Moses. R.A.M.C. replaced by Lt. Cohen. R.A.M.C. (Notes). On night of 17/18th 1/210th Infantry Brigade was relieved by 119th Inf. Bde. on the Right Battn. front. Portion of No.1. Section continued work by day on Rt. Bde. Bottom of Brown Line completed. 600 yards. 2. small panels 18th Welsh Regt. worked thereon on Excavation of same line. Nos. 2 & 4 Sections continued wiring Rt. Bde. front. Brown Line. 1000 yards wire with gaps. completed. 1 Platoon. Works Company & Sappers continued filling of CRATER. on GOUZEACOURT ROAD. No. 3. Section continued work on diversion of TORTILLE. 1 Platoon. digging open portion of same. This diversion ran through the dome top of an old well. Major Miles returned to Company from Hospital. Lt. Branham proceeded on leave to England. 1 Officer (Capt. Pitts). 20th Middlesex Regt. a 10 O.R.s 1/210th Bde. Works. Coy. attached to Company.	PMS
	18.			

Army Form C. 2118.

WAR DIARY
or
INTELLIGENCE SUMMARY.

(Erase heading not required.)

April 1917

Place	Date	Hour	Summary of Events and Information	Remarks and references to Appendices
FINS.	19th	—	Work continued on main Defensive line, Right Bde. Work carried on deepening well in FINS.	TWM
do	20th		Work continued on main Defensive line. Work started on further quarters in FINS. Lt Carr returns from leave.	TWM
do	21st		As on 20th: work on well stopped. Strength 7 Officers 207 OR Attached 3 do 188 OR do 1 do 7 OR Hospital 1	TWM

Army Form C. 2118.

WAR DIARY
or
INTELLIGENCE SUMMARY.
(Erase heading not required.)

April 1917.

Place	Date	Hour	Summary of Events and Information	Remarks and references to Appendices
FINS.	22	—	1 section working in FINS. Half section at crater, two sections preparing to construct Bde H.Q.S. half sections on main line of Defence	T.W.M.
do	23		1 sect working in FINS. 1 Section on crater, ½ section forward dumps, ½ Section main line of Defence. 1 Section on crater. 1 section on Bde H.Q.S. Labour Coy. 1 Platoon on crater. 1 Platoon on Bde H.Q.S. ½ Platoon in FINS, ½ platoon main line 100 Infantry on main line	T.W.M.
do	24th		2 sections wiring captured positions. One section Bde H.Q.S. One section in FINS. all hilum Coy Dumping	T.W.M.
do	25th		2 sections wiring, captured positions. One section Bde H.Q.S. One section in FINS. Two Platoons labour Coy R.E.	T.W.M.

WAR DIARY or INTELLIGENCE SUMMARY

Army Form C. 2118.

(Erase heading not required.)

April 1917

Place	Date	Hour	Summary of Events and Information	Remarks and references to Appendices
FINS	26th		One section wiring Reserve position. One section in FINS. Two section half day salving timber. One section half day on 6 Crater. Labour Coy. Two platoons carrying for wiring parties; with a few men cutting round crater on FIFTEEN RAVINE. One platoon salving timber (half day). One platoon half day on crater.	
do	27th		Infantry. 100 men digging Communication Trench. 5.0 m wiring Reserve position. Mobile charge sent up to Right Battalion to blow up Gemma Craters. Water Explorent, Party highly successful. Reserve wiring. One section culvert etc in FINS. two sections troops, syphons, culvert etc. Left Battalion.	T.M.H T.M.M
do	28th		3 Platoons Labour Coy carrying Hurdal works Bde O.P. Coy carrying Reserve position and front of wire. CRE goes round Reserve position close by Coy work. Appreciation expressed on work done by Coy in wiring and one Bde HQ	T.M.M

Strength. 7 Officers. 206 O.R.
Attached. 3 " 193 O.R.
Hospital. 1 " 3 O.R.

WAR DIARY
or
INTELLIGENCE SUMMARY

Army Form C. 2118.

April 1917

Place	Date	Hour	Summary of Events and Information	Remarks and references to Appendices
FINS.	29th		Two sections wiring front line, one section manning Reserve line, one section in FINS. Trees cut down 'FIFTEEN' RAVINE. Labour Coy comprises	TWM
do	30th		do on 29th.	

W Mitchell
Major RE

CONFIDENTIAL

2nd Field Coy. R.E.

Vol 12 War Diary

From:- 1st. May. 1917.
To. :- 31st. May. 1917.

Volume 12.

Army Form C. 2118.

WAR DIARY
INTELLIGENCE SUMMARY.
(Erase heading not required.)

May 1st/6 1917

Place	Date	Hour	Summary of Events and Information	Remarks and references to Appendices
FINS.	1st		One platoon Infantry started work on DESSART WOOD Crater on FINS — GOUZEAUCOURT road. Fifty men working on Communication Trench alongside GOUZEAUCOURT — VILLERS — PLUICH Railway. 2½ Sections R.E. + 3 Platoons, 121 Bde Labour Company wiring front of Right Brigade: 380 YR single bag put out, and 400 YR renewed from one bag to two. Trenches marked out for Infantry advanced dump of wire started. 2 drivers, 2 horses, report Rollway Travelling Cay at ETRICOURT. 20 men Labour Coy two advanced Battalion Headquarters. Started work on Elephant cupola for B du Headquarters. Started work on Infantry on DESSART WOOD Crater. One platoon Infantry on FINS Crater.	TWM
do.	2nd		Fifty men working on communication trench. One full and two half sections R.E. wiring: three platoons Labour Coy carrying: wire fence completed along Brigade front. 600 screw pickets and 120 coils barbed wire sent up to form forward dumps in event of offensive operations. 20 men Labour Coy Rollway Travelling Coy, Work on GOUZEAUCOURT well carried on.	TWM

located.

11. The 224th Field Company R.E. will be located in the Ravine in R.19.d. and be prepared to move forward to consolidate the position gained on receipt of orders from O.C. 12th Bn S.W.Borderers.

Army Form C. 2118.

WAR DIARY
or
INTELLIGENCE SUMMARY.
(Erase heading not required.)

May, 1917

Place	Date	Hour	Summary of Events and Information	Remarks and references to Appendices
FINS	3rd	—	Continued work on craters and communication trench, Battn Headquarters and Bde Headquarters. Two half sections R.E. wiring: three platoons labour. Cpl forming forward O.P. mnt. 300 pickets and 70 coils barbed wire allotted and up. Work on GOUZEAUCOURT HEAD pushed on.	
FINS	4.	1 am	Received orders for offensive operations on 5th inst; Cpls attached verbally that offensive operation was again cancelled.	A.
		10.15 am	Heard that cancellation was again cancelled.	
		10.20 am	Heard from Bde major 119 Inf Bde that the operation did not	
		12.30 pm	Heard from C.R.E. as to arrangements at permanent occupation of LA VACQUERIE.	
		3 hrs	Received detailed instructions from C.R.E. as to carrying on further work at cellars in LA VACQUERIE.	
		7 hrs	Brigade conference and on road on LA VACQUERIE.	
			Continued work on craters communication trench, Battn. Headquarters and Brigade Headquarters. Work on GOUZEAUCOURT well pushed on by night as well as by day and pump erected. Small party thickening wire.	Ever

WAR DIARY
or
INTELLIGENCE SUMMARY.

Army Form C. 2118.

May 1917

Place	Date	Hour	Summary of Events and Information	Remarks and references to Appendices
FINS.	5th	—	Making up dump for road improvement of villa FINS. Fitting up Pump at GOUZEAUCOURT. Pump recovering but little water coming up. Continuing. Brigade Headquarters sent over with Infantry, photos ready "X" Two parties separate report attached. VAC QUERIE field, Grantham returned from leave.	
FINS.	6th	—	Continuing GOUZEAUCOURT from well. Continued fitting elephant shelter for Bde H.Q.S. Spitlocking out Camps (B rooms) line and mess CT to front line. Improvement to villa FINS. Bulk of labour Coy filling crater on FINS GOUZEAUCOURT road.	Officers O.R. 6. 208. 1. 3. 4. 210 TW as

Strength of body (sick) Hospital. A Macleod

WAR DIARY
INTELLIGENCE SUMMARY

Army Form C. 2118.

MAY 1917

Place	Date	Hour	Summary of Events and Information	Remarks and references to Appendices
FINS.	7th		Orders and lorries Roads in FINS completed and handed over to Transportation. No. 3 Section looking over front line work. Support line and communication latter by Trench marked out and spitlocked. Work commenced on latter by Company and half of the Yorks. Pioneers. No. 2 Section continued work on Well. Pump now running. Water from Well still unsatisfactory. Pump House erected and shelter for men built. No. 4 Section marked out new heads of the Brown line. No. 1 Section continued work in FINS on Billet Improvement and Pumps. Major Miller proceeded on leave to England.	
Do	8th		No. 3 Section & part of No. 4 Section continued work on part of front line. Wiring. Spitlocking & completing portions already dug. Working parties found by Front Battalion & Battalion in close support. Remainder of No. 4 Section continued work on Brown line. Working parties found by Supporting Battalion. 2 Platoons Works Company employed	

Army Form C. 2118.

WAR DIARY
or
INTELLIGENCE SUMMARY.
(Erase heading not required.)

MAY 1917

Place	Date	Hour	Summary of Events and Information	Remarks and references to Appendices
FINS.	8th	—	No. 2 Section continued work on well in GOUZEAUCOURT. Debris cleared from water outfall and to depth of 6' below water surface, by new bourreau. Brown Pipe line reconnoitered from Well to FIFTEEN RAVINE. No. 1 Section continued work on Billet Improvement & Bath House started in FINS. Reinforcement 1 O.R.	
	9th		Work continued on new front line & Communication trench. Parties found as before. 1 Platoon Works employed as Carrying party. Work continued on BROWN LINE & Brown Line Work on Wells & Pipe line continued. Work in FINS on Billet Improvement & Bath House continued.	
	10th		Work continued on new front line. Parties found as before. Work continued. Brown line & Brown as before. Work continued on Wells. New bourreaus made for Brigade Headquarters. Work continued on Billet Improvement & Bath House in FINS.	

WAR DIARY
or
INTELLIGENCE SUMMARY.

(Erase heading not required.)

Army Form C. 2118.

MAY 1917.

Place	Date	Hour	Summary of Events and Information	Remarks and references to Appendices
FINS.	11th		Work continued on new Front Line. Parties as before. Work continued on Communication trench. Working parties working on Brown Line and Mill Brulet. No. 2 Section continued work on Well and Pipe line. Shelter and screening walls over pump house erected. Bund Line being added to water. Pump only delivering 80 gallons of water per hour. Work continued in FINS. Billet Improvements & Bath House. Pte. Reid Black proceeded on leave to England.	
do.	12th		Nos. 3 & 4 Sections continue wiring front line & supervision of Infantry digging party. No. 2 Section work commenced on Water Pond in FINS. Building brick standings for Horses and water carts. No. 1 Section continued work on Bath House & Billet Improvements.	

Strength / Coy.   Officers ORs
                        6   209
Attached   3   200
                    —   —
                    1   2
Hospital

Army Form C. 2118.

WAR DIARY
or
INTELLIGENCE SUMMARY.
(Erase heading not required.)

MAY. 1917.

Place	Date	Hour	Summary of Events and Information	Remarks and references to Appendices
FINS.	13.		Work continued on New Line & Communication trench. 2 Platoons Works Coy. carrying wire.	
	14.		Work continued on Brown Line. Work continued on Water trough & Water point in FINS. Work continued on Bath House, FINS. Work spillocking & wiring on new Front Line continued. Work continued deepening & firestepping new Front Line. Work continued on communication trench & Yffen Ravine forward. 2 Platoons Works Coy. carrying. Work continued on Brown line & Mill trenches. 2 Platoons Works Coy. employed. Work continued on Bath House FINS. & No. 2 Water Point. FINS. Brigade Headquarters Record Boards commenced to-day.	
	15.		Work on new Front Line continued. Work on Communication trench from Yffen Ravine forward. Intermediate line joined through to GOUZEAUCOURT. — CAMBRAI Rd.	

Army Form C. 2118.

WAR DIARY
or
INTELLIGENCE SUMMARY.
(Erase heading not required.)

Mar. 1917

Place	Date	Hour	Summary of Events and Information	Remarks and references to Appendices
FINS.	15th		Work continued on Mill borer.	
			Bath House FINS completed.	
			Work commenced on 2 Nissen Huts for Field Ambulance FINS.	
			Water point FINS completed.	
			Brigade Headquarters Second Wood finished.	
			Work commenced on New Site for Brigade Hdqrs. also Stookwood.	
			Work commenced on No. 4 Water Point FINS – GOUZEAUCOURT Rd.	
			1 O.R. returned from leave to England.	
do.	16th		Wiring & spit locking of new front line completed.	
			Work commenced on present front line. several Bays dug out	
			to proper sections to be finished on pattern for system.	
			Shelters & accommodation for Infantry & boy. Hdqrs on line employed.	
			Work on Brown line continued – Mill borer cont used.	
			Work continued on New Brigade Hd. Qrs.; No. 4 Water Point. Mason	
			Hut for Field Ambulance. 2 O.Rs. Reinforcements.	
			1 O.R. rejoined on discharge from Hospital. 3. O.Rs. attached for Rations.	

WAR DIARY or INTELLIGENCE SUMMARY

Army Form C. 2118.

May 1917.

Place	Date	Hour	Summary of Events and Information	Remarks and references to Appendices
FINS.	17th		Work continued on Tram line. Drainage & pumping of trenches taken in hand.	
			Work continued on Brigade Hd. Qrs. No. 4 Water Point.	
			Camouflage of FINS - GOUZEAUCOURT Road from the direction of HAVRINCOURT.	
			Work commenced on Brigade Lewis Gun & Grenade School. EQUANCOURT.	
			13. O.Rs. detached for Returns.	
			1 Officer (Sec. Lt. K. J. FISHER) 7/10 R. Reinforcement.	
	18th		New communication trench started on left of Sector.	
			Work throughout Sector consolidation reduced by minor operations on right of Brigade front.	
			Work continued on Tram line, Trolley & Camouflage of Road, &.	
			No. 4. Water Point in New Brigade Hd. Qrs. Broad wooden Horse Stalls at Field Ambulance FINS erected. Beds required is complete.	
			No. 99395. Lee Cpl. Keatley, wounded. Class. E.	

Army Form C. 2118.

WAR DIARY
or
INTELLIGENCE SUMMARY.
(Erase heading not required.)

May 1917.

Place	Date	Hour	Summary of Events and Information	Remarks and references to Appendices
FINS.	19th	—	Work continued on front line & communication trenches. Shelters commenced for accommodation for Infantry. Work continued on Brown Line, camouflage of Road, filling in of Mill broken, No 4. Hales Pond. Work continued. Beds for Field Ambulance. 1. O.R. proceeded on leave to England. Company Strength. Officers. 7. O.Rs. 212. Attached. 3. O.Rs. 189. Hospital. — O.Rs. 2. Leave. 2. O.Rs. 1.	
	20th		Work continued on front line system & communications. Continued Brown Line, Roads, camouflage & No. 4. Hales Pond. Work commenced on 119th Brigade M.G. & Bomb School. Work continued Field Ambulance & Billet Improvement. FINS. 1. O.R. admitted Hospital.	

WAR DIARY
INTELLIGENCE SUMMARY

Army Form C. 2118.

May 1917

Place	Date	Hour	Summary of Events and Information	Remarks and references to Appendices
FINS	21st	—	Work continued Front Line & Communication Trenches & drainage of same. Work on Brown Line. Craters, Brigade Hd. Qrs. & No. 4 Water Point continued. Camouflaging of FINS Road requires hackening. Billet Improvement in FINS.	
	22nd	—	Work on Front Line & Communication trenches had to be stopped 12.45 a.m. owing to minor operations. Work on Brown Line, Craters, & No. 4 Water Point continued. Infantry working parties only worked one half of day, owing to Brigade relief. 30 Beds made for 136th Field Ambulance. Huts & extension now complete. Billet Improvement continued in FINS. Major Miller returned from leave to England. 9th to 19th 1917.	M.W.

Army Form C. 2118.

WAR DIARY
or
INTELLIGENCE SUMMARY.
(Erase heading not required.)

May 1917

Place	Date	Hour	Summary of Events and Information	Remarks and references to Appendices
FINS.	23d.		Work continued on front line systems, Brown line Craters at N° 4 Water Point; also Bde Headquarters. Camouflage CAMBRAI Road. Commenced work in conjunction with A.T. Coy on well near GOUZEAUCOURT Stn.	TWM
do.	24th		Work started on ETRICOURT Water Point. Commenced shifting horse-lines from Sugar Factory. Bde Headquarters horse lines settled in new site; grazing ground marked off. Two majors killed. FINS Commenced. Work continued on front line system, B mew line, Crater Water Points at ETRICOURT and FINS (No 4), Camouflaging CAMBRAI Road, well at GOUZEAUCOURT.	TWM
do.	25th.		Work started on Dind Contour DESSART WOOD. Extension of FINS Cemetery commenced. Other work as before.	TWM

WAR DIARY or INTELLIGENCE SUMMARY

Army Form C. 2118.

Place: FINS
Date: 26th May 1917

Summary of Events and Information

Recommenced work on Brigade School, EQUANCOURT. Repairs to well in lines of C/178 Battery, R.F.A. FINS. Of new two changes from well and from water system GOUZEAUCOURT. Completed Canteen, DESSART WOOD. Continued work on FINS Cemetery. Watering point at FINS and ETRICOURT, billet for Town Major FINS, alter billets, camouflaging FINS Town CAMBRAI Road, improvements.

Received intimation of award of Military Medal to No. 99207 Corpl. (acting A/Sergt.) A. JENKINSON for the following act of gallantry and devotion to duty:— On the night of 5th/6th March, 1917, Sergt. JENKINSON showed great coolness and devotion to duty, although heavily shelled and fired on by the enemy, he shewed great devotion to duty in placing charges and letting off attps.

Strength of company
                            O.R.
                            213
attached   7
Hospital   3   191
Leave   1   3
                                    1

Army Form C. 2118.

WAR DIARY or INTELLIGENCE SUMMARY.
(Erase heading not required.)

May 1917

Place	Date	Hour	Summary of Events and Information	Remarks and references to Appendices
FINS.	26th	—	O.C. Sewers wrote on Brown Line and GOUZEAUCOURT Switch by C.R.E.	TWM
do	27th	—	Marking out work on Brown Line and GOUZEAUCOURT Switch and arranging parties and stores. Work on No.4 Watering Point held up owing to lack of transports. Other work as before.	TWM
do	28th	—	Work started on a) Brown Line — digging portion immediately west of CAMBRAI Road and putting out Markers, b) GOUZEAUCOURT Switch — digging trenches, erecting barricades, cutting loopholes in walls, and putting out wire c) Erecting White Huts at rear of skeleton in broken portion of QUEENS CROSS — GOUZEAUCOURT Road. Received report that new well at GOUZEAUCOURT appeared from manner about it of being a failure. Completed No.4 Water Point near DESSART WOOD other work as before.	
do	29th	—	Continued work as on 28th including marking out portion of GOUZEAUCOURT Switch outside the village. Commenced shifting power gear from present well GOUZEAU-COURT to new well.	TWM

WAR DIARY or INTELLIGENCE SUMMARY

Army Form C. 2118.

May 1917

Place	Date	Hour	Summary of Events and Information	Remarks and references to Appendices
FINS	29th	-	Continued wiring Brown Line and started shelters for machine Gun Personnel. Commenced roofing shelters in Sunken Road. Repair work to huts at D.H.Q.	
FINS.	30th		Work continued as before. Recommenced work on Brewery Hts FINS. Commenced clearing ground at new well GOUZEAUCOURT - TVM. Commenced road at new A.R.P. DESSART WOOD	
FINS.	31st		No 1 Section - Recreation of Mixer Hut at Divnl Headquarters FINS. MANANCOURT. Fitting up billet for 9 recovery station. Completion of billet for Town Major, FINS. Completion of Water Point, ETRICOURT. Constructing bunk for Baths, FINS. No 2 Section - Camouflaging FINS - GOUZEACOURT Road	

WAR DIARY
or
INTELLIGENCE SUMMARY.
(Erase heading not required.)

Army Form C. 2118.

May 1917

Place	Date	Hour	Summary of Events and Information	Remarks and references to Appendices
FINS	31st	—	Fitting up well, GOUZEAUCOURT. Construction of shelters in Sunken Road. Fitting up Brigade Hdqrs NURLU. Assisting in sinking well at GOUZEAUCOURT station. No 3 Section — GOUZEAUCOURT Switch line — Fixing up wire entanglements, loopholing walls, building traverses, putting up new buildings advanced of railway station. Assisting RAMC in N° 4 Section — Brown line — machine Gun Emplacements, Shelters and Wire. Q mines and trenches — Completing billet FINS. Fitting up Bde School, NURLU. 121 NB myrule Works Coy. 7 men DONCASTER DUMP. 12 men road at arm Refilling Point. 12 men ETRICOURT Water Point. 12 men deep dugouts for Small Arms Ranges Section. 18 men helping on Brown line. 4 men on GOUZEACOURT Well. Remainder on GOUZEACOURT Switch	TM 9

WAR DIARY
INTELLIGENCE SUMMARY

May 1917

Infantry Working Parties — 4 offs 150 men on Brown Line.
1 off 25 men on shelters in sunken Revd Road 1 off 25 men on crater on FINS — GOUZEAUCOURT Road

T.W.A.

T.W. [signature]
Major R.E.
O.C. 224 Field Coy/R.E.

The 119 Inf Bde is to occupy LA VACQUERIE and hold it for two hours during which time as much damage as possible will be done to the defences and accomodation there.

The Boundary lines between the 119 Inf Bde and the Bdes on either side are

R 26 b 12 — R 21 c 0.0 — R 22 a 0.0 — R 22 a 50.35 — R 22 b 00.55

and
R 20 a 8.7 — R 15 c 0.4 — R 15 d 7.3 — the road thence past the church to R 16 c 1.4 — R 16 c 7.3.

12th S.W.B will attack on the Right and 17th Welsh Regt on the Left.

Parties will be formed as under

No 1 Party under Lt Carr – 10 men from No 1 Section + 20 men 13th Yorks Regt (Labour Coy)

No 2 Party under Lt Power – 10 men from No 4 Section + 20 men 20th Middlesex Regt (Labour Coy)

Parade at 7.30 pm and move up to front line trenches.

Dress – Rifles, 50 rds s.a.a., bayonet, water bottles filled, haversack rations.

Tools Per Party.
    2 Shovels
    1 short crowbar
    3 wire cutters
    1 hammer
    2 folding saws
    3 electric torches.

The men of the Labour Company will each carry one made-up charge and one P Bomb.

The RE Parties will follow the Infantry into no mans land and will form up behind the 119 Trench Mortar Battery, lying down until the barrage lifts. They will then follow the moppers up into VACQUERIE and will move to the road turning at R15 d 7.2.

Here Lt Carr's party will move along the road round the turning at R15 d 8.4 to the road junction near the church and destroying cellars of all houses on the right of the road and any in the space between the roads.

Lt. Power's party will destroy all houses on both sides of the road leading from R 16 c 00.05 to R 16 c 15.40 and will then

Having completed their task they will in retiring blow down any buildings in their area until their explosive is destroyed. P bombs to be thrown into cellars.

Special care must be taken to bring back all wounded and dead before the parties withdraw. If there are too many to be dealt with the first will be carried clear of VACQUERIE while the stretchers return for the remainder.

When all explosive is exhausted, parties will withdraw on the order of the senior: the latter will report to major ANDREWS, 17th Welsh Regt. near the cross roads at R.21.b.6.5. that all his men including wounded have been withdrawn. Major ANDREWS' position will be marked by a red lamp.

The recognition mark between the men of the RE parties will be 'RE DONCASTER'.

Headquarters.
119th Infantry Brigade.

Report of operations on LA VACQUERIE.

Some fifteen charges laid and fired in village on Right Flank. (R.16.c.2.4.). Actual destruction obtained doubtful: but several houses damaged.
Remaining charges could not be fired owing to proximity of our own troops. 2 dugouts fired with P. Bombs.

6. 5. 1917.

Headquarters.
119th Infantry Brigade.
C.R.E. 40th Division.

Further report on Operations 5th & 6th.

Two parties (each 1 Officer. 11. O.R. R.E. 21. Infantry Coy. & 2 Stretchers.). Formed up in the Ravine at R.19.d. and collected their explosives there about 10 p.m. They moved up to the front line trenches forming up in rear of the "moppers up." attached to 17th Welsh Regt. who were formed on a tape in No man's land.

They reached their position about 10.40 p.m. Immediately the Barrage lifted they conformed to the movements of the troops in front, who advanced at once. At this point one of the carrying party was wounded.

The parties reached the wire in front of LA VACQUERIE. about R.15d.9.1. at 11.30 p.m. but as the Infantry had overrun their barrage the left party withdrew about 200 yards under instructions from the Infantry. When the Barrage lifted the wire in front was found to be insufficiently cut and Capt. GOFF 17th Welsh Regt.

sent back a message asking the Artillery to do this.

The attackers lying down meanwhile in the open.

This caused a delay of about 3/4 of an hour. so that it was 12.15 a.m. before they entered the village at R.15.d. 9.1. being at this time under heavy fire. from Rifles. Machine Guns & Bombs. from their right front and right flank. Just before crossing the wire the parties passed through the 119th Trench Mortar Battery. The parties here separated.

(a).

Lt. CARR'S party now proceeded to the houses at R.15.d. 9.3. and laid charges in three houses and a dugout under a house. during which operation a damaged gable was brought down. At this time the party met Capt. GOFF and some men of the 17th Welsh Regt. in the road and he asked that no charges be fired until his men were clear. The enemy at this time were firing at, and Bombing, the party from the big farm at R.16.c.2.4 strength estimated at about 30. About this time the "moppers up" were observed retiring through the wire and the continual activity of the enemy forced the R.E. party to withdraw. It was then too late to fuze the charges but half a dozen P Bombs were thrown into a dugout. About 12.50 a.m. the party withdrew through a belt of uncut wire during which they were under heavy fire and Sapper Reasbeck was severely wounded in the chest.

On clearing the wire the party

met MAJOR ANDREWS. reported to him and withdrew, reaching our own trenches about 1.30 a.m. While passing through the enemy barrage. CORPORAL WATERLOW was wounded.

(b.) Lt. POWER'S party proceeded to the Northern edge of the village where they met Capt. GOFF who warned them that they were in a very exposed position. Acting on his advice the party proceeded to the Eastern edge of the village and attacked a large residential house at. R.16.c.15.20. with portable charges and P. Bombs. The house was damaged but the total extent of the damage could not be observed. Two German bodies were observed hanging out of the upper windows. The remaining charges were laid outside the walls of the house at R.16.c.10.10. The houses were severely damaged. The party during this time was under fire (rifle & machine gun) from the Orchard R.15.c.20.15. but were covered by men of the 17th Welsh Regt.

The party then retired down the main street, assisting the Infantry to remove a wounded man. They reached our trenches about 1.25 a.m.

A. Stretcher Bearer was mortally wounded by a machine Gun Bullet from the East while returning from LA VACQUERIE to our trenches.

Observations

The fact that the Infantry were held up by wire so that the parties were only in LA VACQUERIE half an hour accounts for the small amount of damage actually done. There was no time for reconnaissance or for searching for cellars and the party was under close fire most of the time.

The great difficulty seems to have been the lack of information as to the location of our own troops, and of the enemy, which materially hampered movement.

I think both the Officers (Lieut. CARR and Lieut. POWER) showed considerable energy and skill in handling their parties and the N.C.Os. (Sergt. JENKINSON, Corporal WATERLOW & Corporal MUSSON) were indefatigable in their efforts. Capt. Goff 17th Welsh Regt. gave valuable assistance to the parties both in the way of information and of protection. His coolness & skill were specially remarked.

All the men both of the 224th Field Company & 121st Brigade Labour Coy. behaved with extreme coolness & steadiness throughout the operations in face of very considerable difficulties.

Technical notes.

Each carrier carried one P. Bomb and one Mobile charge. The mobile charges were composed of 5 slabs of Guncotton in a wooden Box with a fuze to burn 5 minutes. The fuzes were lit by matches, as the fuze lighters had not proved satisfactory.

Before the party started, the Carriers were told off, two carriers to each Sapper, to know one another by name. The following tools were carried by each party.

    2 Shovels.
    3 Wire Cutters.
    2 Folding Saws.
    1 Hammer.
    1 Short Crowbar.
    3 Electric Torches.

Confidential

Vol 13

WAR DIARY

224th Field Co R.E.

Vol 13

JUNE 1917

22nd L
Comp
War
from Ju
to Ju
Vol

WAR DIARY or INTELLIGENCE SUMMARY

Army Form C. 2118.

Place	Date	Hour	Summary of Events and Information	Remarks and references to Appendices
FINS	June 1917	1ᵃᵐ	Work continued viz:-	
			No.1 Section — Erecting Nissen huts at ETRICOURT, fuel refining, marking of many tracks.	
			Station FINS; fitting up bathhouse at SOREL, making road for ammunition Refilling Point DESSART WOOD	
			No.2 Section — Shifting well at GOUZEAUCOURT, renewing FINS - GOUZEAUCOURT Road, erecting shelters in Sunken Road.	
			No.3 Section — GOUZEAUCOURT Sentab, constructing ads. of many Stations for R.A.M.C.	
			No.4 Section — Brown line. 119 Bde dohore NURLU	
			121 Works Coy. — ETRICOURT Water Point, Brown line, ARP DESSART WOOD, GOUZEAUCOURT WELL, GOUZEAUCOURT Sentab. Left — 15.0 m Brown line, 2.5 m craters, 2.5 m shelters	
			G.S.O I moved GOUZEAUCOURT Sentab to select M.G. E.O.	TWM

Army Form C. 2118.

WAR DIARY
or
INTELLIGENCE SUMMARY.
(Erase heading not required.)

June 1917

Place	Date	Hour	Summary of Events and Information	Remarks and references to Appendices
FINS	2nd		Work as on 1st. Punk shifted to new well GOUZEAUCOURT to B be Relief.	TW 2
FINS	3rd		No Infantry Working Parties continued as before. 1.R.E. and Works Coys. Septfilled in at PETRICOURT and Water Point 9 mt up. Strength of Coy. in am. Officers 7. attached 3. Hospital 1. FIELD Leave. 1.	O.R.s. 2/55 2/11 2 2 TW 3
FINS	4th do		No Infantry Working Parties. Transportation and reall GOUZEAUCOURT Work as before.	TW 4
FINS	5th		Infantry (21st Middlesex Regt) started work as follows:- 50 on GOUZEAUCOURT duties 25 on Mill Crater 25 on GOUZEAUCOURT Crater 25 on shelters in one sunken Road 25 on shelters in another sunken Road	

Army Form C. 2118.

WAR DIARY
or
INTELLIGENCE SUMMARY.
(Erase heading not required.)

June 1917

Place	Date	Hour	Summary of Events and Information	Remarks and references to Appendices
FINS	5th		50 am Road for A.R.P. DESSART WOOD 125 (about) on B new line. Works Company relieved of A.R.P. got and trench relief started on shelters for tunnel R.mg. Section.	
FINS	6th		Brown hew between FINS — GOUZEAUCOURT and HEUDICOURT — GOUZEAUCOURT roads — 35% of trench completed. Wire completed to one bay and 70% completed to two bays. 4 Machine Gun Emplacements completed.	

Army Form C. 2118.

WAR DIARY
or
INTELLIGENCE SUMMARY.
(Erase heading not required.)

June 1917

Place	Date	Hour	Summary of Events and Information	Remarks and references to Appendices
FINS	6th		GOUZEAUCOURT Switch: wire 80%; trenches 60%; Barricades 80%; Loopholes 45%; MG Emplacements 6 under construction	TWM
			New well GOUZEAUCOURT - Pump wanted, shelters under construction. Infantry company in three craters.	
			Sunken Road Q.33.a.8. 7 complete, 1 partially complete, 2 shelters partially erected. 3 excavations partially complete. dug-out shelters partially erected.	
			Shelters in Sunken Road R.31.a. 3 partially covered.	
			Bath House SOREL 90% complete.	
			Bath House NURLU Work commenced	
			Field Survey Coy - 3 Latrines completed to depth FINS completed	
			136 Field Ambulance - Extensions to present construction	
			Advanced OR dressing Station - 3 under construction	
			137 Field Ambulance - 2 Macun Huts complete	
			Road to New Rifling Point - 150' complete	
			Wire sent to 181 Bde. R.F.A. to await with 2 reports for OPs TWM	

WAR DIARY or INTELLIGENCE SUMMARY

Army Form C. 2118.

(Erase heading not required.)

June 1917

Place	Date	Hour	Summary of Events and Information	Remarks and references to Appendices
FINS	7th		Work continued as before. Pumping started at GOUZEAUCOURT — pumping only delivering 60 galls per hour	T.W.M.
			F.S.C. Gyaxtra - Churchway commenced	T.W.M.
	8th		Return to map at Field Ambulance MANANCOURT - had before as before 3 men sent to keep it clean in Hospital	
	9th		Work continued as before. Started sinking GOUZEAUCOURT dustbin outside village and began new M4	T.W.M.
			Explosives up at GOUZEAUCOURT again set of extra chain benches and pulley hoist sent at GOUZEAUCOURT at 119 Bde school NVRLU continued	
			Erection of mess huts. Started Camouflaging OP up to at FIFTEEN RAVINE angle on experiments officers. Strength of Coy attached Hospital 5 leave.	T.W.M. 7 3 194
			by TIN POT TRACK. Repaired SOREL Watering Ponds.	
	10th		Central work as usual up to 12 noon when Infantry Coys completed party at GOUZEAUCOURT status huts. B now hive. Completed Bath house SOREL Completed Camouflaging OP post at FIFTEEN RAVINE.	T.W.M.
			Started work on 30 yds Range in Quarry near FINS. Completed wire in GOUZEAUCOURT village	

WAR DIARY
or
INTELLIGENCE SUMMARY.
(Erase heading not required.)

Army Form C. 2118.

June 1917

Place	Date	Hour	Summary of Events and Information	Remarks and references to Appendices
FINS	11th	—	No Infantry Working Parties. Works Company concentrating on A.R.P. DESSART WOOD. One Platoon Works Coy. resting. Forming up first shelter of Dugout for Field Survey Coy. Crossings of Road and Railway on TIN POT TRACK completed. Two more in hand.	
FINS	12th		Infantry Battn. (11th + Kings Own) started work as following:- 175 men constantly shelters behind BROWN LINE 25 men on MILL CRATER 25 men on GOUZEAUCOURT CRATER } Filling in Craters 25 men on I. GOUZEAUCOURT Sw. CRATER 25 men on one Sunken Road, 25 men on another overhead shelters 50 men on GOUZEAUCOURT SWITCH — sandbagging and clearing 50 men (H.L.I.) on road to A.R.P. Works Company — One platoon resting. 20 men on dugouts for Sound Ranging Section 30 men on 30 yrd range FINS. 19 on TIN POT TRACK + Sunken Road 13 men on GOUZEAUCOURT Sw. Crater. 4 men on Brewery Well 4 men on private Baths FINS. 11 men on new Dumps	

WAR DIARY or INTELLIGENCE SUMMARY

Army Form C. 2118.

June 1917

Place	Date	Hour	Summary of Events and Information	Remarks and references to Appendices
	12th		R.E. — No.1 Section Returns to Field Ambulance, MANANCOURT: 120 th Inf Bde School, NURLU: 30 yd ramp FINS; erecting shed for the clerks at Baths, FINS: erecting tank for disinfecting water at SOREL: preparing accumulators for new Drinking pump. Painting signs. No.2 Section — Completing fitting of well and pump, GOUZEAUCOURT, searching for and repairing new wells in GOUZEAUCOURT, erecting shelters in sunken road, repairing TIN POT TRACK, to FINS GOUZEAUCOURT. No.3 Section — Erecting shelters for machine guns in GOUZEAUCOURT SWITCH, enemy barrage at GOUZEAUCOURT crater, intermittently during to FINS GOUZEAUCOURT STN CRATER. No.4 Section — making out works on BROWN LINE, erecting shelters in Sunken Road. Detailed from Sections:— No.1 Section — R.E. Dump 1, dump Ranges, No.2 Section, sinking well Work 3 ————— Section 1, Agricultural ————— level Railway Section 1, GOUZEAUCOURT ind E+M Camp 8, level Railway Station GOUZEAU R.A.O.P. 4, Pumping station GOUZEAU COURT 2 —————	

WAR DIARY
INTELLIGENCE SUMMARY

June 1917

Place	Date	Hour	Summary of Events and Information	Remarks and references to Appendices
FINS	12th	—	No 3 Section - advanced Dressing Station 3 No 4 Section - 119 Bde School NURLU 6. Total 29	TWM
	13th		Excavating shelters which Brown knew Enlarging walls and erecting M.G. shelters in GOUZEAUCOURT Erection of Tanks in GOUZEAUCOURT Clearing top of B tramway well GOUZEAUCOURT three waters, and started work on continued work on move. Revetting and starting shelters in two dukers Roads completed one room at 119 Bde School NURLU one shelter and one third another at F.S.C Dugout Framed one chamber and one Gangway Stairs under RE aufnahme. R.A.M.C. constructing three ador ARP DESSART WOOD - 20 Y.R. lane in day is making road at ARP DESSART WOOD - 20 Y.R. lane in dag. Excavating deep dugouts for 189 Bde R.F.A. O.P. - Two entrances and half chamber complete. Repairs to TIN POT TRACK. Fanning funny front at 30 yd range FINS.	TWM

WAR DIARY or INTELLIGENCE SUMMARY

Army Form C. 2118.

June 1919.

Place	Date	Hour	Summary of Events and Information	Remarks and references to Appendices
FINS	13th		Clean clothing store FINS Baths completed. Erecting new G.I. urinal G.I. workshop started work on frame Baths. FINS. Painting names at villages in G.I. enamel. Taking down NISSEN Huts for use of 120 Inf. Bde. Completing baths at NURLU. Erecting tanks for water supply at SOREL. Total 26 jobs. Arranging for working parties from 35th G.I. coys. to work on these water points.	
FINS	14th		Started work on three Water Points: each party, 1 off. 30 other ranks, 2 bakers. One party completed 35 YR having without middle top and did considerable amount of earth filling and 13 YR having with middle top. Washing baths from 14th H.L.I. Roofing one shelter behind Brown Line, and excavating others.	

WAR DIARY
or
INTELLIGENCE SUMMARY

Army Form C. 2118.

June 1917

Place	Date	Hour	Summary of Events and Information	Remarks and references to Appendices
FINS	14th		Completed second Mess Room at 119 Bde school and withdrew Working Party. Framing up Johnson Bath FINS. Restarted Camouflaging of CAMBRAI Road. Other work as before.	
			Warned to send 1 off 100 o.r. Works Company to dig cable Trenches under O.C. 31st Div beyond B Coy. Received intimation from 136 Field Ambulance that water from well GOUZEAUCOURT only required one measure Chloride of Lime.	TWM
FINS	15th		Excavating and roofing dilletos and digging down on Brown L. sandbagging walls GOUZEAUCOURT switch. Both parties on one W.P. by mistake. NURLU Water Points – B oth shewn. 52 Y.R. HEUDICOURT Water Point – Continued brushing along trough. Work delayed by lateness of waggons	

WAR DIARY
INTELLIGENCE SUMMARY

(Erase heading not required.)

Month: June 1917.

Place	Date	Hour	Summary of Events and Information	Remarks and references to Appendices
	15th		TIN POT TRACK complete. 119th Bde School NURLU complete. 120th Bde School NURLU complete. Both Horse lines NURLU & FINS - reframes completed. One advanced dressing station through Clear Clothing store FINS Baths complete. NISSEN Huts for 120 Bde - 10 Taken down, being erected exit of side at SOREL. Completed Hutments of camp named SOREL. Working Parties found by 14th A.S.H.	TW 2
FINS	16th		Took 25 men off GOUZEAUCOURT SWITCH and started them on craters on GOUZEAUCOURT - LEPAVE Road. State of shelters in Lehu Road, QUEEN'S CROSS - 2 Elephants complete, 5 shelters complete, 5 nearly complete, 2 just started. ditto GOUZEAUCOURT - 1 complete, two nearly, one felt, one and a half excavated, two nearly finished, one roofed. Shelters in Brown line - One completed, one roofed, one being roofed, 2 ready for framing, 6 being excavated. Lt. Fraher went down near Brown	TW 2 17th S/L 2/Lt 13

Army Form C. 2118.

WAR DIARY
or
INTELLIGENCE SUMMARY.
(Erase heading not required.)

June 1917

Place	Date	Hour	Summary of Events and Information	Remarks and references to Appendices
FINS	17th		Started work clearing trees on GOUZEAUCOURT – CAMBRAI Road. Organised party for R.A.O.P. for 181 Bde R.F.A. complete. Marquee taken down. Brownings Well, reporting about six feet of rubbish on a tablet platform in. Break down of plant sinking well at GOUZEAUCOURT in.	TWM 1
	18th		Working parties from 114 East Surrey Regt. 104 Bde at NURLU. No working parties from. Water Pumps. Clearing trees on GOUZEAUCOURT – LE PAVE Road. 1 man. Working party out to GOUZEAUCOURT Well to control names.	TWM 2
FINS	19th		Very heavy rain storm causing big collapse in GOUZEAUCOURT wells, and minor collapses in other contours.	TWM 3

WAR DIARY or **INTELLIGENCE SUMMARY**

Army Form C. 2118.

June 1917

Place	Date	Hour	Summary of Events and Information	Remarks and references to Appendices
FINS.	20th	—	Working parties from 10th Gloucester Regt (35 th Division) start work as follows:-	
			Water Point at HEUDE COURT	
			30 men — Water Point between NURLU and MANANCOURT	
			30 men — Water Point between NURLU and SOREL	
			30 men — Water Point between NURLU and FINS – GOUZEAUCOURT Road	
			180 men — Broad gauge line South of FINS – GOUZEAUCOURT Road	
			No working parties from Infantry 40th Division	
			No 1 Section – Erecting Messa Huts and making hypo for horses and making out Japanese Baths, NURLU	
			No 2 Section – Erecting Shelters in sunken road, screening of Japanese Baths, FINS; Running wall to Main Road; Erecting Japanese Baths at GOUZEAUCOURT.	
			No 3 Section — Erecting Shelters in sunken road workshops	
			No 4 Section — N3 annex line Shelters erecting Japanese Baths FINS.	

Army Form C. 2118.

WAR DIARY
or
INTELLIGENCE SUMMARY.
(Erase heading not required.)

June 1917

Place	Date	Hour	Summary of Events and Information	Remarks and references to Appendices
FINS.	20th		Working parties:- 100 men on Cable Trenches under 40th Div and Brigade. 7 men Strength Q m Stores. 14 men on GOUZECOURT walls, 9 men on deals dugouts, 6 men assisting camouflaging one Japanese Baths. FINS. Water Pound completed. HEUDECOURT Water Pound 7). 12th SWB (117th Inf Bde) started work as follows:-	WLM
FINS	21st		Working parties from 12th SWB (117th Inf Bde) started work as follows:-	TW2
		1 off 20 OR }	Three parties filling craters of ——— CAMBRAI Road	
		1 off 20 OR }		
		1 off 20 OR }		
		1 off 20 OR }	Excavating for shelters and two bunker Roads	
		1 off 20 OR }		
		1 off 50 OR	Making road to ARP DESSART WOOD	
		2 off 90 OR	Brown line North of FINS-GOUZEAUCOURT Road	
			Instructed to start work on a) Q and Bomb Store near DESSART WOOD b) Making out camps. Instructed to suspend work on Japanese Baths, FINS	

WAR DIARY or INTELLIGENCE SUMMARY

Army Form C. 2118.

June 1917

Place	Date	Hour	Summary of Events and Information	Remarks and references to Appendices
FINS	22nd		Work continued as before. Parties found by 18th Welsh Regt. Work on GOUZEAUCOURT Stn. Craters interfered with by shell fire. the SIMMS. No 3 Station recently unmasked.	TW M
FINS	23rd		Started work on two more wells in GOUZEAUCOURT. Instructed to install elephant shelters outside D.H.Q. Dugouts to make up dugouts taking place for 119 Inf. Bde., 3 Rifle. DESSART WOOD Dugouts. Work continued as before. Parties found by 19th R.W.F. Work on F.S.C. Dugouts practically completed. Same three weeks. 2 R.E., 6 to 20 workers daily, up to 12 hrs. one week day. Started work on Permanence of Water Supply between NURLU and MANANCOURT completed. Water Point between FINS and SOREL started. Water Point between FINS and SOREL started. Three new men agents for proposed enemy Theatre near FINS. Reconnaissance for proposed enemy Theatre near FINS. FINS Three depots reported as shops.	O.R. T.2/3 3.171 3. Hunting Boy. Washer. Hospital. Leave. 7 TW M
FINS	24th		Started work on a) Refreshment to DESSART WOOD Shelters complete Cinema Theatre FINS. b) Elephant shelters in CROZIER LANE Water Point between NURLU and SOREL complete	TW M

Army Form C. 2118.

WAR DIARY
or
INTELLIGENCE SUMMARY.
(Erase heading not required.)

June 1917

Instructions regarding War Diaries and Intelligence Summaries are contained in F. S. Regs., Part II. and the Staff Manual respectively. Title pages will be prepared in manuscript.

Place	Date	Hour	Summary of Events and Information	Remarks and references to Appendices
FINS	24th		Expt. Nissen Hut completed for Reserve Brigade. Two bangalore torpedoes filled. Loading out unloading ancillary. F.S.C. Dugout complete.	T.W.M.
FINS	25th		2 Nissen Huts drawn for RAMC FINS. 14th Gloucesters completed their period of employment under R.E. Work generally very good. Bomb store started, roofed. Quarters moved well in SOREL, which have been blown up by enemy. Railway cutting by enemy. Bangalores to 119 Inf Bde. Sergeant explaining out corps. Marking out new Nissen huts.	T.W.M.
FINS	26th		Started work on new Nissen huts.	

WAR DIARY or INTELLIGENCE SUMMARY

Army Form C. 2118.

June 1917

(Erase heading not required.)

Place	Date	Hour	Summary of Events and Information	Remarks and references to Appendices
FINS.	27th		Well at GOUZEAUCOURT started by hanging weights on bottom halves. Output raised from 70 gallons per hour to 350 gallons per hour.	TWM
			C.R.E. inspecting sites of huts. 1 Elephant shelter complete at new DHQ (35/6/2m). Party of H.L.I. working on Brown line and FINS water point.	
FINS	28d		Considerable work on monkey and helmet camps. Moison hut FINS complete. C.R.E. states 35th Q warm. Received notification from and that 121 Inf Bde would be being withdrawn.	TWM

Army Form C. 2118.

WAR DIARY
or
INTELLIGENCE SUMMARY.
(Erase heading not required.)

June 1917

Place	Date	Hour	Summary of Events and Information	Remarks and references to Appendices
			take over frontage, 224 Coy to work in this section. C.R.E. points out site for new D.H.Q. Huts at SOREL.	TW_M
FINS	29th		O.C. arranging with O.C's 204 and 205th Field Companies from taking over work. Work started on new Osmul H.Q. 100 men guards to latter. Batts awaiting late alterations arrangements to wiring Gang to take over work of 203 Field Coy 14/6 Capt Smith arranging	

WAR DIARY
or
INTELLIGENCE SUMMARY.

Army Form C. 2118.

June 1917

Place	Date	Hour	Summary of Events and Information	Remarks and references to Appendices
FINS.	30th		Site of new DHQ shifted to a site North of SOREL.	Officers. ORs.
			Strength of Coy.	7 213.
			Attached.	3. 169.
			Hospital.	2.
			Leave.	10.

M. Mulley
Major RE
O.C. 224th Coy RE

Vol 14

Confidential

WAR DIARY

224th Field Coy RE

July 1917

WAR DIARY
INTELLIGENCE SUMMARY

(Erase heading not required.)

Army Form C. 2118.

July

Place	Date	Hour	Summary of Events and Information	Remarks and references to Appendices
HEUDECOURT	1st		Company moved individually from FINS HQS. moved Section and No 3 + 4 Sections from FINS to HEUDECOURT. No 1 and 2 Sections to VILLERS GUISLAIN. 2 Platoons Works Coy. moved to Railway Cutting behind VILLERS – GUISLAIN, remainder still at FINS. No 3 Section carrying on Divnl HQS at new site ordered to have out huts complete inclusive of those already erected by enemy. 2nd Batho. FINS and on No 4 Section on Japanese Camp.	
do.	2nd		2 Sections on DHQ SOREL. Work held up owing to incomplete huts being sent up by carts. Work started in hoe on dugout Infantry winning	TWM

Army Form C. 2118.

WAR DIARY
or
INTELLIGENCE SUMMARY.
(Erase heading not required.)

July 1917

Instructions regarding War Diaries and Intelligence Summaries are contained in F. S. Regs., Part II. and the Staff Manual respectively. Title pages will be prepared in manuscript.

Place	Date	Hour	Summary of Events and Information	Remarks and references to Appendices
HEUDECOURT	3rd		Work as before. 1 platoon Works Coy moved to BOX DUMP. Seven huts now erected at new D.H.Q.	
do	4th		Work in front line on deep dugouts, shelters, drainage.	
do	5th		Work as before. Remainder Works Coy moved up from FINS.	
do	6th		Work as before. D.H.Q. moved from MANANCOURT to SOREL.	

WAR DIARY
or
INTELLIGENCE SUMMARY.

Army Form C. 2118.

July 1917

Place	Date	Hour	Summary of Events and Information	Remarks and references to Appendices
HEUDECOURT	7th		Restarted work on baths at FINS and NURLU. Started erecting shelter in front line system two rifle ranges near HEUDECOURT.	
				Officers O.R.s
			Strength of bn. 7. 212.	
			Attached. 2. 159.	
			Leave. 15	
			Hospital. 2.	TW L
do.	8th		Work as before	TW M
do	9th		Work continued on Q and HQs. Japanese huts FINS; Japanese Baths NURLU. Marking out camps, completion of excavation of four mined dugouts, erection of tank shelter in support line; erection of one gate, marking out new tank. R.A.M.C. aid Post VILLERS – GUISLAIN.	TW N

Army Form C. 2118.

WAR DIARY
or
INTELLIGENCE SUMMARY.
(Erase heading not required.)

July 1917

Instructions regarding War Diaries and Intelligence Summaries are contained in F. S. Regs. Part II. and the Staff Manual respectively. Title pages will be prepared in manuscript.

Place	Date	Hour	Summary of Events and Information	Remarks and references to Appendices
HEUDECOURT	10th		1 Coy Pioneers moved to VAUCELETTE FARM for work on trenches.	Two
			Pioneers started work on front line near TURNER QUARRY but stopped work early. Infantry mostly wiring, clearing trenches, drawing bays, trenchwards and building fire bays.	
			Nos 1 & 2 Sections VILLERS-GUISLAIN — Monkey sub tunnel shelters, drawing trenches, erecting French gates. Exactly Russian sap for rally post completely advanced. Gwernsey Station camouflaging. Working on former deep dugouts.	
			No 3 Section Working on Brnd Headquarters SOREL	
			No 4 Section completing Infantry baths, NURLU and FINS.	

Army Form C. 2118.

WAR DIARY
or
INTELLIGENCE SUMMARY.
(Erase heading not required.)

July, 1917

Place	Date	Hour	Summary of Events and Information	Remarks and references to Appendices
HEUDECOURT	11th		Work as before including erection of shallow dugout at Right Battn Headquarters.	
do	12th		100 Corps cavalry reported for work in Camps - 50 at HEUDECOURT, 30 at NURLU. Work started on D.A.C. Camp NURLU and Battn Coy DESSART WOOD. Work started on camouflaged trench to M.G. Emplacement TWENTY-TWO RAVINE. Two dugout completed. Camouflaging TWENTY TWO AVEN complete.	TWM
do	13th		Work as before two rifle ranges HEUDE COURT.	

Army Form C. 2118.

WAR DIARY
or
INTELLIGENCE SUMMARY.
(Erase heading not required.)

July 1917

Place	Date	Hour	Summary of Events and Information	Remarks and references to Appendices
HEUDECOURT	14		Camouflaging CEMETERY ROAD complete. Tramway completed in SPUR TRENCH. Started work on Monastery at FINS. British Cemetery Strength of Coy. Officers 7. ORs. 212. Attached. Officers 2. ORs. 159. Hospital 5. Leave. 1. Officer 12 ORs.	
HEUDECOURT	15th		Forward billets in VILLERS - GUISLAIN heavily shelled. Three casualties. No 99311 Sapper TURPLIN G.H. mortally wounded. No 107196 2/Cpl BROOME L.T. severely wounded. No 99310 Spr. FOUL STONE C.E. slightly wounded (returning to duty). No 107033 Lee Cpl DOWNS A. accidentally injured while working on a dug-out. Started making out new support line between STORAR AVENUE and FAWCUS AVENUE.	
do.	16th		Tramway complete. Clearing of Front line East and South of TURNER QUARRY, and start work on TWENTY TWO AVENUE. Trench cutting GEORGE ST filled in & bridged	

WAR DIARY or INTELLIGENCE SUMMARY

Army Form C. 2118.

Place	Date	Hour	Summary of Events and Information	Remarks and references to Appendices
Hendecourt	16th July 1917		Erecting tents, shelters in support lines. Improvements to Battn HQ.S.	

No 3 Section.
Taking down Nissen huts at SOREL and re-erecting at Cav. Workshop store. Box DUMP and Q in 6 H.Q.S. Erecting twenty minor additions to FINS at FINS British Cemetery. New pipe line Water Point searching four German pipe lines. PEIZIERE.

No 4 Section.
DESSART WOOD. Erecting Camps as follows a) for 1 Battn Infantry complete. (Two Nissen Huts complete, 2 Cookhouses complete all latrines excavated, one partially erected.) b) for Pioneer Battn Two Nissen Huts complete, two cookhouses complete all latrines excavated, one latrine erected, two latrines partially erected. c) D.A.C. Camp

WAR DIARY or INTELLIGENCE SUMMARY

Army Form C. 2118.

July 1917.

Place	Date	Hour	Summary of Events and Information	Remarks and references to Appendices
HEUDECOURT	17th	—	Work started by one Coy. Pioneers on new supports line between STORAR AVENUE and FAWCUS AVEN. Work in hand. No 1 Section – Deep dugouts for Coy. Headquarters (in hand), Batts Headquarters (40 F.R. approximately). Shallow dugouts at Batt. Headquarters VILLERS-GUISLAIN (nearing completion). New advanced O.P. near station (Well in front – has tank (communication) bomb proof), but work later abandoned. Shelters for opening up, HIGH ST. (three weatherproof complete). Supports in front line (three shelters complete to date). Shelters in front line (new supports making one in hand). Minor repairs, start of works on new supports to STORAR AVEN. B. myside O.P. ROBERTS AVEN. out and superintending drainage dump. Pumping station. Front line forward dump. Control of forward dump. No 2 Section. Two deep dugouts for Coy. H.Q.S. Jolly point Avenue front line trench through own line. (Reveres dep 35 F.R complete.)	

WAR DIARY or INTELLIGENCE SUMMARY.

Army Form C. 2118.

Place	Date	Hour	Summary of Events and Information	Remarks and references to Appendices
HEUDECOURT	July 1917		3 Mess Hut complete, 1 Mess Hut partially complete & Cookhouses complete: all latrines excavated, half latrines erected. a)Sgts mess Cook - one Mess Hut complete, 2) Above shower constructed mess hut. b) Artillery Bde Wagon Lines - being built. One Mess Hut partially erected, all latrines excavated. Lt. Fisher marking out additional camps, and superintending Eng Workshop and Painters shop. 121 Bde Works Coy Australy RE especially on dug dugouts and shelters, acting as guides as newry. Australy at new O.C. HQS at Mentraing. Improving two Rifle Ranges HEUDECOURT. Revetting trenches at Physical Training School, SORREL. Constructing Coverny Place over Granville line	

Army Form C. 2118.

WAR DIARY
or
INTELLIGENCE SUMMARY.
(Erase heading not required.)

July, 1917.

Place	Date	Hour	Summary of Events and Information	Remarks and references to Appendices
Hendecourt	17th		III Corps Cavalry (100mm) Working with No. 4 Section on dugouts, half at NURLU, half at DESSART WOOD. Pioneers Z Coy working on - connecting front line round TURNER QUARRY. Digging TWENTY TWO AVENUE. Digging camouflaged exit out to TWO AVENUE. Digging camouflaged exit out to TWENTY TWO RAVINE. Machine gun Pioneers - new support line. X Coy working on - new support line.	TWM
	18th 19th		Work continued as before	TWM

WAR DIARY
INTELLIGENCE SUMMARY

(Erase heading not required.)

July 1917.

Place	Date	Hour	Summary of Events and Information	Remarks and references to Appendices
HEUDECOURT	19		Instructed to prepare to commence work on T.M. Emplacements in front line. Fine stripping of VIEW TRENCH started. Camouflaged net to machine Gun Emplacement TWENTY TWO RAVINE complete.	TWM
HEUDECOURT	20		III Corps Cavalry withdrawn. Lilly hole for Right Batter complete (54 ft long) approximate note of advance as Reserve Lap 4'×2' 9' for 24 hours, 9' top of well in front. Restarted work on cutting away top of well in front his trench Hut SOREL started Church Army Hut SOREL started Mortars 9' FINS new Batted Cemetery complete & removal Headquarters complete & steps for camouflaging.	TWM

WAR DIARY
or
INTELLIGENCE SUMMARY.

July 1917.

Place	Date	Hour	Summary of Events and Information	Remarks and references to Appendices
Heudecourt	21/6		Church Army Hut, SOREL completed.	
			Went round with O.C. 121 T M Batty to fix sites for	
			Stokes Guns.	
			Started marking out sites for Bde. Transport	TWM
			lines on FINS — HEUDECOURT Road.	
			Strength of Coy.	Officers. O.R.s
				7. 208.
			Attached.	2. 100.
			Hospital.	1. 6.
			Leave.	1. 2.

Army Form C. 2118.

WAR DIARY
or
INTELLIGENCE SUMMARY.
(Erase heading not required.)

July 1917

Place	Date	Hour	Summary of Events and Information	Remarks and references to Appendices
HEUDECOURT	22nd		C.R.E. gang round to settle new support line from CIRCUS SWITCH to CROOK QUARRY	
			No 3 Section relieves No 2 Section in left Battn. sector	
			Two dugouts for Coy Headquarters (for Centre Left Coy, Right Battn and Left Coy Left Battn) completed and off GEORGE STREET	
			Front line between FAWCUS AVENUE and STORAR AVENUE heavily bombarded with Heavy T.M's and new dugout now well shelled.	
			Started work on Ammo Dump Dugout in Gunn Line	Two
			Officer exiled to new tunnel from CHESHIRE QUARRY to TWENTY TWO AVENUE to form second exit from Dugout in CHESHIRE QUARRY	Two

Army Form C. 2118.

WAR DIARY
or
INTELLIGENCE SUMMARY.
(Erase heading not required.)

July 1917.

Instructions regarding War Diaries and Intelligence Summaries are contained in F. S. Regs., Part II. and the Staff Manual respectively. Title pages will be prepared in manuscript.

Place	Date	Hour	Summary of Events and Information	Remarks and references to Appendices
Quesnoy	23rd		Started work on 2 Stokes Trench Mortar Emplacements in Old Front line behind SPUR TRENCH. Making out trench round CHESHIRE QUARRY in conjunction with 178 Tunnelling Coy R.E.	TWM
	24th		Started wiring new support line. Started new Garage at D wood H.Q.S. new G average at D wood H.Q.S. Trench connected up to BICESTER ALLEY. TWENTY TWO AVENUE. Pioneers started work on trench round CHESHIRE QUARRY. Started work on making out line of new dugout line in country to C.R.E.'s instructions. Hauling over two camps (Infantry Batt.n and Pioneer Batt.n) near DESSART WOOD to 231 Coy R.E.	TWM TWM TWM

WAR DIARY or INTELLIGENCE SUMMARY

Army Form C. 2118.

Place	Date	Hour	Summary of Events and Information	Remarks and references to Appendices
HEUDECOURT	25th July	11 pm	Word received of probable enemy raid in early morning 26.7.17. Arranged to warn out withdraw working parties.	
			Started work on Nether Trench motor Emplacements.	
			FAWCUS AVENUE. Started work on FAWCUS AVENUE — 3 x 3 dugout. Line cut through to final dimensions. About half completed.	TWM
			Following cars in hand:— ① D.A.C. NURLU (Winter) ② Quint Town NURLU (Winter) — GOUZEAUCOURT Road (Summer) ③ Artillery Bde FINS — GOUZEAUCOURT Road (Summer) ④ Artillery Bde Transport Lines DESSART WOOD (Summer) ⑤ + ⑥ Infy Bde (Summer) ⑦ + ⑧ 2D ACs (Summer) ⑨ + ⑩ Artillery Transport Lines (Winter) HEUDECOURT Road. Bde Wagon Lines FINS — HEUDECOURT Road.	TWM

Army Form C. 2118.

WAR DIARY
or
INTELLIGENCE SUMMARY

(Erase heading not required.)

Place	Date	Hour	Summary of Events and Information	Remarks and references to Appendices
HEUDECOURT	26th	6am	13th Yorks raided by enemy. Finally heavy casualties. Enemy artillery had down in our Front line trench no 6-8 Front on a company front and raiding party entered ally undamaged. Raiders got no floor an incomplete dugout in FAWCUS AVENUE, where portion of garrison had taken shelter, and severed majority of their Prisoners. There Both Companies of wool Rs were put on keeping up trenches — one company on front line, one company in FAWCUS AVENUE. Trenches rendered passable before him Bells in VILLERS - GUISLAIN shelled in barrage No.1 Section took out cart blown up by a bit. Evening of trench Elephant shelter at Left Batten H.Q.S complete. Restarted camouflaging of HIGH STREET	

WAR DIARY
INTELLIGENCE SUMMARY

July 1917

Place	Date	Hour	Summary of Events and Information	Remarks and references to Appendices
Heudecourt	26th		Started work on extra TM Emplacement near TWENTY TWO RAVINE. O.C. ninth Brigade major 121 Inf Bde settling line of new support line between CIRCUS SWITCH and FIFE ROAD in accordance with ideas of 40C Brigade. Orders received that all work on advanced OP near Station to be abandoned. VILLERS – GUISLAIN — Shell proof protection complete.	TM"

WAR DIARY
or
INTELLIGENCE SUMMARY.

Army Form C. 2118.

Place	Date	Hour	Summary of Events and Information	Remarks and references to Appendices
Jenlecourt	27-	July	2 Coy Pioneers continuing clearing front line trenches through LEITH WALK. 2 Platoons Y Coy Pioneers cutting new support line to connect up new support line. Reconnoitring for possible sites for shelters — will – front. GUISLAIN: One Dugout at GEORGE ST complete. Trenching of Dugouts at FIFE ROAD complete. Dugout for Coy Headquarters at FIFE ROAD complete. Five stepping VIEW TRENCH SWITCH commenced. Five stepping CIRCUS SWITCH commenced. Work proceeding on following huts. ① D.A.C. men — Huts complete ② Amb all accessories and 10 men 5" men Hats complete T m NURLU — all accessories ③ ④ Infy Bde Transport 3 men Huts under erection 6 latrines partially lines — 6 latrines erected, 6 latrines partially erected, 1 latrine partially erected ⑤ arty Bde Wagon lines all latrines complete, 2 under construction ⑥ artry Bde Wagon lines — Material supplied to erect	TWN TWN

WAR DIARY
or
INTELLIGENCE SUMMARY

Army Form C. 2118.

(Erase heading not required.)

July 1917

Place	Date	Hour	Summary of Events and Information	Remarks and references to Appendices
Neuve ----	28th		2 Platoons Y Coy O.M.C. Training anywhere by day in front line cleaning and resting. Two Platoons in support by night on new support line. (two of) O.C. reviewing and reinforcing new supports line between CIRCUS SWITCH and FIFE ROAD. No 9922 Cpl ROPER wounded by machine gun fire while in charge of working party. Attached on Leave. Hospital.	TW_M Officers 7 O.R.'s 208 155 4
	29th		d.R.E. round front line trench from STORAR AVENUE to DENNING AVENUE. Quiet Line continue work on Front line for another day. Y Coy N	TW_M TW_M

WAR DIARY
or
INTELLIGENCE SUMMARY.
(Erase heading not required.)

Army Form C. 2118.

July 1917.

Place	Date	Hour	Summary of Events and Information	Remarks and references to Appendices
HEUDECOURT	30th		2 Coy Pioneers ordered to stop work on connecting BICESTER ALLEY to BROADHURST AVENUE and to start work on new support line North of CIRCUS SWITCH.	TMs
do.	31st		Work of Company. No 1 Section – Working in trenches in VILLERS – GUISLAIN Sector. Working on :- new ammunition Reserve store LEITH WALK; (12 F R chamber excavated; Stokes T.M. Emplacement off FAWCUS AVENUE (clearing trench, work rather uncertain owing to uncertainty of T.M.O. as to site); fixing 4 beds in each of two deep dugouts vestry near S Elephant shelters in front and support lines; excavating and framing shallow dugout at Right Battn Headquarters (now 100 ft long). Running R E Dump and Power Pump in VILLERS — GUISLAIN.	

WAR DIARY
or
INTELLIGENCE SUMMARY.

(Erase heading not required.)

Army Form C. 2118.

July, 1917.

Place	Date	Hour	Summary of Events and Information	Remarks and references to Appendices
Havrincourt	3d		No. 3 Section — Working in GAUCHE Sub sector Trenches Employed on — Three Stokes TM Emplacements (1). Emplacements and Recess complete Shelter in hand (2). 22 TR Camouflaged of Work started on Gun Emplacement complete. (3). Gun Emplacement excavated being framed. Clearing trench leading to it). Erecting small elephant shelter in Supports hine. Camouflaging HIGH STREET Cutting drains. Repairing five steps in new supports hine. Opening up new Markey out new supports hine in Right well in VILLERS-GUISLAIN.	
			No. 2 Section. Wiring new Support hine in Right Battn Sector. Preston between STORAR AVENUE and FAWCUS AVENUE complete. Erecting Garage & Camp Stables for Divnl Headquarters Partholong. Camp Commandants Officers Hut.	

WAR DIARY
INTELLIGENCE SUMMARY

Army Form C. 2118.

Place	Date	Hour	Summary of Events and Information	Remarks and references to Appendices
Neulette	31st		No 4 Section — Employed on Camps. (1) D.A.C. Camp NURLU 10 men Huts complete, 6 under erection (2) 9 wd Tram NURLU & men Huts complete (3) Lty Bde Tramway lines SOREL all latrines separated, eight latrines new erected. (4) Artillery Bde Wagon Lines 7 meters Huts erected. (5) Artillery Bde Wagon Lines Muttencourt Huts erected. Wagon Lines making out Camps applied. 2 Lt. Fisher, C.S.M. and a few men employed with R.E. on dugouts, shelters Works, log-hutting. Also on rifle ranges and Physical Training School SOREL (resetting trenches everyday cookhouse, everyday shed).	

July. 1917.

Army Form C. 2118.

WAR DIARY
or
INTELLIGENCE SUMMARY.
(Erase heading not required.)

July 1917

Place	Date	Hour	Summary of Events and Information	Remarks and references to Appendices
HEUDECOURT.	31st		Girial Pioneers Z Coy working on Support line left Battn 175 Y R of trench 3 x 3 dug from CIRCUS SWITCH night 30th - 31st. Dutch Trench round CHESHIRE QUARRY dug for 100x. Y Company working on different lines Right Battn, portion between STORAR AVENUE and FAMOUS AVENUE; Half dug to complete dimensions (front to 3' x 3'.

Location of Coys - Headquarters, Wagon Lines, and Nº 2 and 4 Sections at HEUDECOURT. Nº 1 & 3 Sections VILLERS GUISLAIN.
121 Bde Works Coy - Headquarters and ½ platoon HEUDECOURT 1 Platoon RAILTON. 2½ platoons VILLERS - GUISLAIN.
Coy Dumps - Box 9 nr RAILTON, and advanced dump, VILLERS GUISLAIN. | |

T.W. Miller
Major R.E.
O.C. 224 Field Coy R.E.

Confidential

War Diary
of
224th Field Coy R.E.

From 1st August 1917
To 31st August 1917

Volume 15

Army Form C. 2118.

WAR DIARY
or
INTELLIGENCE SUMMARY.

(Erase heading not required.)

August 1917

Place	Date	Hour	Summary of Events and Information	Remarks and references to Appendices
HEUDECOURT	1st	9am	Received orders to hand over Right Battalion front to 35th Division and to take over our battalion front from 229 Field Company R.E. Moved O.C. 204 Field Coy R.E. moved here. Both Companies Pioneers working in support line between CIRCUS SWITCH and FIFE STREET all parties ordered to be clear of trenches by 12 midnight to avoid enemy retaliation after raid. Section to take over from 229 Field Coy R.E.	
do.	2nd	—	Went round GONNELIEU. No. 4 Section (A. Power) relieves No. 1 Section (L. Cooper) in VILLERS GUISLAIN	

Army Form C. 2118.

WAR DIARY
or
INTELLIGENCE SUMMARY.
(Erase heading not required.)

August 1917

Place	Date	Hour	Summary of Events and Information	Remarks and references to Appendices
HEDECOURT	5th		Completed pile line from Water point to Baths	
	6th		Completed survey of new support line between CIRCUS SWITCH and FIFE ROAD. Completed two trench mortar emplacements. Strength of Coy: Officers 2, O.R. 208, Attached N.R. Coy. 154, Prisoners 6	

WAR DIARY or INTELLIGENCE SUMMARY

Army Form C. 2118.

August 1917

Place	Date	Hour	Summary of Events and Information	Remarks and references to Appendices
HEUDECOURT	14th		Practising with 12th Suffolk Regt. Bangalore torpedoes in conjunction with 12th Suffolk Regt. two Platoons with were successful results. 18' got in each case.	
			5. ORs which in Hospital; evacuated a Strength of Coy.	Officers O.Rs. 7 207 Attached Works Coy. 2 153
	18th		Hospital Leave Strength of Coy. Attached Works Coy. Hospital Leave	— 1 — 3 Officers O.R. 7 150. 2 OR. 205. — 14 — 4
do	19th		Party of No.4 Section went out to lay Bangalores in enemy wire. Owing to enemy having working party out the attempt had to be abandoned.	

WAR DIARY
or
INTELLIGENCE SUMMARY.

Army Form C. 2118.

(Erase heading not required.)

August 1917

Place	Date	Hour	Summary of Events and Information	Remarks and references to Appendices
HEUDECOURT	20th		10.O.R. reinforcement arrived	TWM
	22nd		1.O.R. reinforcement arrived	
do.	26th		Two Bangalores had applied to 12th Suffolk Regt and fired by No 4 Section in enemy wire. Result not observed	TWM

Army Form C. 2118.

WAR DIARY
or
INTELLIGENCE SUMMARY.

(Erase heading not required.)

August 1917

Place	Date	Hour	Summary of Events and Information	Remarks and references to Appendices
HEUDE-COURT	29th		Started class in anti-bagging for officers and N.C.O.s	HEUDE TWY

do	31st		Started work on new Bde HQS.
			
			 Strength of Coy. Officers ORs
			                      7 204
			       Attached 2 150
			       Hospital — 3
			       Leave — 7
				TWY

W. Mully
Major RE
O.C. 224 Field Coy RE

Vol 16 Confidential

War Diary

of

204th Field Coy. R.E.

From 1st Sept 1917

to 30 Sept 1917

Vol. No. 16

WAR DIARY or INTELLIGENCE SUMMARY.

Army Form C. 2118.

(Erase heading not required.)

Instructions regarding War Diaries and Intelligence Summaries are contained in F. S. Regs., Part II. and the Staff Manual respectively. Title pages will be prepared in manuscript.

September 1917.

Place	Date	Hour	Summary of Events and Information	Remarks and references to Appendices
MŒUVRES	1st		Work on fire as before.	
do	2nd		Work on Brigade Headquarters as before. Work on camps for Divisional tram & Infantry transport.	
do	3rd		1 O.R. evacuated - shown off strength. Strength of Company: 7 Officers, 204 O.R.; Work company 2 Officers, 109 O.R. No.2 Section relieved No.3 section on Right Sub Sector. Other work as before.	
do	4th		Work as before.	
do	5th		Work as before.	
do	6th		1 O.R. evacuated - struck off strength.	
do	7th		Work as before.	
do	8th		do. do. do. Strength of Coy. 7 Officers, 203 O.R.; Work Company 2 Officers, 148 O.R. 1 O.R. rejoined Coy.	
	9th		Raid on German trenches by 13th Yorks Regt. happened in and with Bangalores. Strong enemy patrols encountered, leading to hurried retirement. Two Bangalores and two coils cable lost. No.1 Section relieved No.4 Section on work on Right Sub Sector. Other work as before.	

WAR DIARY
INTELLIGENCE SUMMARY

(Erase heading not required.)

September 1917

Place	Date	Hour	Summary of Events and Information	Remarks and references to Appendices
HEUDECOURT	10th		Work as before.	
do.	11th		Work as before.	
do.	12th		Work as before.	
do.	13th		1. O.R. Reinforcement. Work as before.	
do.	14th		8 O.Rs. reinforcements. Work as before.	
do.	15th		1. O.R. proceeded to Base Depot Rouen as Instructor. Strength of Company. 7 officers. 211 O.R.s.; Work Company 2 officers 8. 147. O.Rs. Work as before.	
do.	16th		Work as before.	
do.	17th		1. O.R. wounded by shell fire. 1. O.R. admitted Hospital "Sick". Evacuated to strength of Company. Work as before.	
do.	18th		1. O.R. evacuated to strength of Company. Work as before.	
do.	19th		2nd Lieut. G.R. CLARK to CRE's office for special work on new camps. 2nd Lieut. K. FISHER takes over No.2. Section. Started work on extension of dugouts, construction of tunnels to M.G. Emplacements.	
do.	20th		1. O.R. evacuated to strength of Company.	

Army Form C. 2118.

WAR DIARY
or
INTELLIGENCE SUMMARY.

(Erase heading not required.)

September 1917.

Place	Date	Hour	Summary of Events and Information	Remarks and references to Appendices
HEUDECOURT	20th	Could	Ordered to send 2 N.C.Os. 16 Sappers to 12th Suffolk Regt. to assist in demolishing enemy work during hours on trenches. Sent from No.3 Section. New Brigade Headquarters completed. Brigadier expressed himself very well pleased.	MM
do	21st		Work as before. Started camouflaged trench along CHESHIRE STREET and Work Company ordered.	MM
do	22nd		Work as before. Dummy raid near GONNELIEU - VACQUERIE Road on evening 25 instant. Land mines to be fired by 223rd Field Coy. R.E. and dummy figures moved by 224th Field Coy. R.E. to attract hostile barrage. Strength of 224 Field Coy. R.E. 7 Officers, 207 O.Rs. Work Company 2 Officers 150 O.Rs.	MM
do	23rd		1 O.R. (attached to 12th Suffolk Regiment) wounded night of 22/23/9/17. Fitting up & intermediating with dummy figures. Work as before.	MM
do	24th		1 O.R. wounded boy from 238th (A.T.) Coy. R.E. Raid GRANTHAM - badly placing dummy figures in NO MANS LAND. Raid on German trenches. Owing to strong hostile resistance, only one dugout was destroyed. Casualties, 1 Sapper missing, believed killed, 2 N.C.O.& 2 Sappers wounded. 1 Sapper shell shock. Dummy raid very successful. Enemy barrage on figures very heavy & several figures completely destroyed.	MM
do	25th		The following was specially good work on the actual raid, another demolition of dugouts; No.49330 Sec Cpl N.WHITE: No.19509 Sapr A.NARD. No.107027. Sapr R. BAYS. Report of O.C. 12th Suffolk Regt. says: "Wish to add that the parties of 223 & Field Coy. R.E. who were attached to my Battalion for the enterprise did splendid work throughout."	MM

WAR DIARY
or
INTELLIGENCE SUMMARY.

Army Form C. 2118.

September 1917.

Place	Date	Hour	Summary of Events and Information	Remarks and references to Appendices
HAVRECOURT	25th	Cont'd	2/Lt. ROBINS M.C. whom I saw after his wound was dressed, was especially emphatic on their good work and gallant behaviour in the close fighting that occurred in BLACK SUPPORT TRENCH. Strength of Company. 7 Officers. 202. O.R., Both Companys. 2 Officers 150. O.R.	
do.	29th		1. O.R. rejoined Coy. from Base.	
do.	30.		1. O.R. rejoined Coy. Gun Boat Store for Right Bank complete.	

P.W. Miller
Major R.E.
O.C. 224 Field Coy R.E.

Vol. 17

Confidential

War Diary

of

224th Field Company R.E.

From: 1st October 1917.
To: 31st October 1917.

Volume 17.

Army Form C. 2118.

Instructions regarding War Diaries and Intelligence
Summaries are contained in F.S. Regs., Part II
and the Staff Manual respectively. Title pages
will be prepared in manuscript.

WAR DIARY
INTELLIGENCE SUMMARY.
(Erase heading not required.)

October 1917.

Place	Date	Hour	Summary of Events and Information	Remarks and references to Appendices
HEUDECOURT	1st		Work in line continued as before. No 3 Section completing revetting of Reserve Trench. No 4 Section working on top of Bde Transport lines. 2 O.R. evacuated and Tank off strength	TWM
do	2nd		Work as before. Arranged to hand in work we have in hand before Q and more Companys to step in.	TWM
do	3rd		M.A.C. TRENCH and GUN SUPPORT. 1 O.R. evacuated and distance off strength. Received orders from Q.M. Work as before. 2 O.R. evacuated and Tank off strength	TWM
do	4th		Work as before.	
do	5th		O.C. 54th Field Coy came up for preliminary reconnaissance.	TWM
do	6th		O.C. 54th Field Coy goes round line to take over. Strength of Coy 7 offrs 199 O.R. Works Coy 2 offs 151 Nos No 3 Section and part of No 4 Section working on Camp for D.R.E. in HEUDECOURT.	TWM

2353 Wt. W2544/1454 700,000 5/15 D.D.&L. A.D.S.S./Forms/C. 2118.

Army Form C. 2118.

WAR DIARY
or
INTELLIGENCE SUMMARY.
(Erase heading not required.)

October 1917

Place	Date	Hour	Summary of Events and Information	Remarks and references to Appendices
HEUDECOURT	7th		No 3 Section moved to new Camp, HEUDECOURT. 4 O.R. rejoined Coy from hospital	TWM
do	8th		No 4 Section moved to new Camp. 52 O.R. attached from Infantry for fatigue work returned to their units.	TWM
			1 O.R. rejoined Coy from hospital	
do	9th		Headquarters moved to new Camp, handing over to 8th Fd Coy. Works Company concentrated and moved to new area. Attachment to 13th Yorks Regt. being killed at VILLERS-GUISLAIN	TWM
do	10th		No 1 and 2 Sections hard at work at HEUDECOURT for shelters and move to extreme front speculation that work on shelters near GOUZEAUCOURT. Preparation start.	TWM
			No 3 & 4 Sections and No 2 & 4 Sections working on	TWM
do	11th		No 1, 2 Sections at work in camp	TWM
do	12th		No 1 & 3 Section shelter	TWM
do	13th		Work as before. Strength 7 offrs 204 O.R.	TWM
do	14th		Work as before. Half day only. Capt DICKIE 14th A.SH. attacked during training in staff work	TWM

2353 Wt W2344/1454 700,000 5/15 D.D.&L. A.D.S.S./Forms/C. 2118.

Army Form C. 2118.

WAR DIARY
or
INTELLIGENCE SUMMARY.
(Erase heading not required.)

Instructions regarding War Diaries and Intelligence Summaries are contained in F. S. Regs., Part II. and the Staff Manual respectively. Title pages will be prepared in manuscript.

October 1917.

Place	Date	Hour	Summary of Events and Information	Remarks and references to Appendices
HEUDECOURT	15th	—	Work as before. 10 R reinforcements found from Base.	TWM
do	16th	—	Work as before. 10 R wounded shell fire.	TWM
do	17th	—	Received verbal orders to move. 18th Parties recalled from work. Fifteen cupolas erected (6 completed with sandbags) at one site, thirteen cupolas erected (8 camouflaged and covered) at the other.	TWM
do	18th	—	Moved to PERONNE. Mounted portion by road, dismounted portion by Decauville from FINS.	TWM
PERONNE	19th	—	Mounted portion marched to BAPAUME (5 offs 1020 R.) Dismounted portion entrained at PERONNE & travelled at SAVULTY, LARBRET, marched to LARBRET (2 offs 990 R)	TWM TWM
LARBRET	20th	—	Mounted portion marched from BAPAUME to LARBRET. Strength of Company. Officers 30+. O.R. Attached 1 officer+3 O.R. (M.O.)	TWM
do	21st	—	Baths and Drill. 40 R reinforcements received.	TWM
do	22nd	—	Drill and T raining. 10 R reinforcements received. Received warning orders to move.	TWM

Army Form C. 2118

WAR DIARY
or
INTELLIGENCE SUMMARY
(Erase heading not required.)

October 1917

Place	Date	Hour	Summary of Events and Information	Remarks and references to Appendices
L'ARBRET	23rd	—	Continued training: drill, musing, foot, coy.	TW M
do	24th	—	Continued training. 4 offrs and 7 NCOs taking part in Bde attack scheme. 1 OR rejoined from hospital.	TW M
do	25th		Capt DICKIE completes attachment to Coy. Continued training.	TW M
do	26th		Continued training, principally company & 3 offrs & 5 NCOs taking part of Bde attack scheme.	TW M
do	27th		Repetition of Bde attack scheme. 3 OR reinforcements received. NCOs with 121 Bde attended. Received orders to send billeting party to move whole company by bus. Ordered to prepare to move. Two centuries train. These orders cancelled, and orders received to move to BAPEAUME & part dismantled. Transport on 28th not to PERONNE by rail but to BAPEAUME by road. Transport on 29th not to remain behind. Completed Company. 7 offrs 210 OR attached 1 off (MO) 3 OR Strength of Company.	TW M
do	29th		Transport (less 2 carts) marches to BAPEAUME.	TW M

WAR DIARY
or
INTELLIGENCE SUMMARY

(Erase heading not required.)

October 1917

Army Form C. 2118

Place	Date	Hour	Summary of Events and Information	Remarks and references to Appendices
L'ARBRET	29th		Transport (less 2 sects) marches from BAPAUME to PERONNE. 2 sections (Nos 3 & 4) march to SUS-ST-LEGER under orders of 121 Inf. Bde. Headquarters and 2 sections (dismounted) entrain at COUY and detrain at PERONNE	
PERONNE	30th		IOR rejoins from hospital. Company (less 2 sections) marches from PERONNE to EQUANCOURT and goes into huts for night	TWM TWM
EQUANCOURT	31st		Company moves into new huts CRE hutment work for Field Companys at FINS	TWM

W. Muller
Major
O.C. 224 Field Coy RE

WAR DIARY
INTELLIGENCE SUMMARY
(Erase heading not required.)

224 Field Coy R.E.   November 1917

Place	Date	Hour	Summary of Events and Information	Remarks and references to Appendices
EQUANCOURT	1st	—	Started work erecting Infantry shelters in FINS with N° 1 & 2 Sections	TWA
do.	2nd		Continued work. Eight shelters completed.	TWA
			N° 3 and 4 Sections working on rifle range	
			Completed accommodation for two Companies (12 offrs,	
do.	3rd		380 O.R.) in FINS. Strength 7 offrs 212 O.R. (2 offrs & 60 R detached)	TWA
do.	4th		Started work in EQUANCOURT — Eight shelters	TWA
			completed	
do.	5th	—	Continued work in EQUANCOURT. Two additional shelters completed.	TWA
do.	6th		Continued work in EQUANCOURT. Seven additional shelters completed.	
			Major Mills proceeds on leave to England, Captain Smith acting O/C.	
			Lieut. Griffith proceeds to Brighton to take up duties of Senior Training Schools Instructor.	
do.	7th		Continued work in EQUANCOURT. Four additional shelters completed	
do.	8th		Continued work in EQUANCOURT. Four additional shelters & 1 Bn. HQ. completed.	
do.	9th		Continued work in EQUANCOURT. Six additional shelters completed.	
do.	10th		Continued work in EQUANCOURT. Six additional shelters completed.	
			Lee. Cpl. Fisher & L.S.M. Lord proceed to Bourges for course of training at III Army Infantry School	
			of Instruction. FLIXECOURT. Strength of Coy. 7 Officers, 210 O.R. (2 offrs. & 83 O.Rs. detached.)	
do.	11th		Continued work in EQUANCOURT. Three additional shelters completed.	
			1 O.R. rejoined Company from Hospital & 1 Coy. HQ.	

Army Form C. 2118

Instructions regarding War Diaries and Intelligence Summaries are contained in F.S. Regs., Part II. and the Staff Manual respectively. Title Pages will be prepared in manuscript.

WAR DIARY
INTELLIGENCE SUMMARY
(Erase heading not required.)

November 1917

Place	Date	Hour	Summary of Events and Information	Remarks and references to Appendices
EQUANCOURT	12th		Continued work as before.	
	13th		Continued work as before. They additional shelters w 1. Coy. H.Q. completed. The tarpaulins used for this work were camouflaged by another camouflage squad finished off. 1. Coy. Hd. Qrs & 1. Bat-n. Hd. Qrs. completed. The shelters same day as they were erected.	BMW
			Strength of Unit in Officers 310 O.R. (Ex Officers Observers)	
	14th		Accommodation for 2000 O.R. commenced (in groups of 200. 1 Coy Hd Qrs (approx. group) at FINS.	
	15th		Work continued. 1st. Company group completed.	
	16th		Work continued as before.	
	17th		Work continued. 2nd Company group completed. in conjunction with work done by other field company. Further base uys Company from leave to England, Baigneux 2000 accommodation was completed in two days. Strength of Coy. 7 Officers, 311 O.Rs. (1. Officer & 21 O.Rs. detached).	
	18th		Warning orders received for move. Company stores & transport unchecked. 1. O.R. admitted to Hospital.	
	19th		Moved from EQUANCOURT to ROCQUIGNY. Transport left 2 sections left EQUANCOURT. 4-15 p.m. arrived ROCQUIGNY. 6-30 p.m. sections Nos. 3+4 rejoined the Coy. from ACHIET-LE-GRAND at 1-30 a.m. the 20th. Major Miller rejoined together from leave. 1. O.R. reinforced from R.E. Base Depot. 3. O.R. admitted to Hospital.	BMW
	20th		Ordered to be prepared to move at one hours notice. Kits dumped. W. Power rejoined from leave. 1 OR to hospital	TW 2

WAR DIARY or INTELLIGENCE SUMMARY

Army Form C. 2118

November 1917.

Place	Date	Hour	Summary of Events and Information	Remarks and references to Appendices
ROQUIGNY	21st	—	Received orders 11 a.m. to move 12.15 p.m. to BEAUMETZ-les-CAMBRAI with 121 Inf Bde Group. Arrived 3.15 p.m.	TWM
BEAUMETZ	22nd		Worked on cross country track from DEMICOURT and to CANAL du NORD, in conjunction with 229 Fd Coy RE to Germans wire completed by 226 Fd Coy RE village. In time to work afternoon. Received orders to be in HAVRINCOURT 23rd. 10R to Hospital, 10R rejoined from hospital.	TWM
HAVRINCOURT	23rd		Left BEAUMETZ 2.10 a.m. advanced centre marched via HAVRINCOURT 8.15 a.m. mounted parties to HERMIES to HAVRINCOURT 10.15 a.m., but horsey to TRESCAULT arriving TRESCAULT owing to marched near No mans land. The leave two horsedrawn wagons near infavourable state of roads. Pontoons were pitched later the same day. The brake or wheel of 1 Pontoon breaking owing to the bad state of the roads. Lieut Carr + 1 N.C.O. proceeded to GRAINCOURT as Liaison Officer to 121st Inf. Bde.	TWM
do			Major Miller slightly wounded by rifle or machine gun Bullet whilst reconnoitring front line in BOURLON WOOD. All 4 sections worked on Strong Points parading H.O.P. m. returning to Billets 5.15 a.m. (35 h.). Strong Points constructed E.18.c.8.B. + E.13.c.7.T. Map. MOEUVRES Special sheet 1/20.000.	WM
do	24th		Strength of Company 5 Officers. 185. ORs. (attached. 1 Officer. 16 ORs.) Leave 1 Off. 13. ORs. Command. 16/1. 4 ORs Hospital. 5. ORs. Detached. 3 ORs.	WM

1875 Wt. W593/826 1,000,000 4/15 J.B.C. & A. A.D.S.S./Forms/C. 2118.

WAR DIARY
or
INTELLIGENCE SUMMARY
(Erase heading not required.)

Army Form C. 2118

November 1917

Place	Date	Hour	Summary of Events and Information	Remarks and references to Appendices
HAVRINCOURT	25th		4 Sections paraded at 5-30 p.m. & worked on Strong Point. E.18.c.3.3. (Map. MOEUVRES. Special Sheet. 1/20,000.) Returned to Billets 11-30 a.m. (26th).	AW
do.	26th		1 O.R. rejoined Company from Hospital. 4 Sections paraded at 11-30 p.m. to work to Strong Point. Bns about. E.23.b.8.8 & one about. E.18.C.3.4. Sections went back by orders of G.O.C. 187th Brigade. 62nd Division top.m. as his line was then in enemy's hands.	AW
do.	27th		4 Sections paraded 4-0 p.m. Sections 2,3 & 4 extended Strong Point at new Strong Point. E.18.b.5.7. (Map. MOEUVRES. Special Sheet. 1/20,000). No.1 Section returned to Billets. 3 a.m. (28th). No.1 Section returned to Billets at 4 a.m. (28th), and passed through a gas shell barrage on returning from work. Also No.2 Section	AW
do.	28th		Company also 1 Platoon 124 Yorks. (Pioneers) (Platoon strength 28.)(Company strength 37). moved from Strong Point in BOURLON WOOD. E.18.B.6.7 to edge of WOOD. Average thickness of entanglement. 5 strands. Wire laced in trees & brushwood. No pickets being used. Party returned 12-50 a.m. (29th). Company showing signs of exhaustion. 47. O.Rs "Sick". No.2. Section. (23. ORs.) been working about 2 hours/on CR.13	AW
do.	29th		Company 1st/2nd No.2 Section rested. No.2 Section continued work on CR12 & Hot. Bn. Bns shells almost completed. 2nd Hully. 50% complete. Work commenced on Roads by 4 Sections. 8-30 a.m. Echoings & tramming - filling of shell holes. road works on HAVRINCOURT- FLESQUIERS. Work commenced at HAVRINCOURT end. all work stopped	AW
do.	30th		by heavy enemy shelling. Orders received from R.P.M. 3rd Division to move all transport clear of south of village.	AW

Army Form C. 2118

WAR DIARY
or
INTELLIGENCE SUMMARY
(Erase heading not required.)

November 1917.

Place	Date	Hour	Summary of Events and Information	Remarks and references to Appendices
HARRINCOURT	30th Novr.		As soon after receipt of orders as possible. Bridging wagons loaded & all wagons packed ready to move. Company ready to move by 3.0 p.m. Warning order received 7-0 p.m. Orders cancelled 10-0 p.m. Strength of Company. Officers. 195. O.Rs. (Attached 1 officer 4 O.Rs.) Hospital. 1 officer 1 O.R. S. O.Rs. Command. 1 officer. 1 O.R. Detached. 3. O.Rs.	[signature]

[signature]
O/C. 22nd Field Company R.E.

Vol 19

Confidential

War Diary
of
224th Sikh a Coy R.E.

From 1st Decr. 1917
To 31st Decr. 1917

Volume No. 19

Army Form C. 2118

WAR DIARY
or
INTELLIGENCE SUMMARY

December 1917.

(Erase heading not required.)

Instructions regarding War Diaries and Intelligence Summaries are contained in F.S. Regs., Part II. and the Staff Manual respectively. Title Pages will be prepared in manuscript.

Place	Date	Hour	Summary of Events and Information	Remarks and references to Appendices
HAVRINCOURT	1st		Warning order received to move on the 4th.	—
do.	3rd		Lieut. A. Grantham proceeded on leave.	—
do.			Capt. E.W. Smith R.E. proceeds to BOIRY BECQUERELLE to take over work from 155th Field Coy R.E. Company sustained casualties 1 O.R. killed 5 O.R. wounded.	—
do.	4th		Column. 1. 2. 3. 4 + a dismounted Headquarters moved by Bus to fillets Section.	—
BOIRY BECQUERELLE			at. T.8.c. 3.3. Sheet. 51. B. S.W. Mounted transport moved to BEAULENCOURT.	—
do.	5th		Major E.F. Martin M.C. R.E. reports for duty and assumes command. Mounded section under Lieut. Cant arrives from BEAULENCOURT.	—
do.	6th		Lieut Bones. Nos. 3 & 4 sections moved to billets in line at T.6.a.6. at T.6.a.6. at for work.	—
do.	8th		Defensive lock for new Intermediate line from T.18.c.80.20. to T.5.b.6.3 sited and work commenced same night.	—
do.	10th		Lieut. G.A. Clark returned from leave to England.	—
do.	13th		1 O.R. reinforcement from R.E. Base Depot. New trench to form defensive flank sited from V.1.c. 25.50. to V.1.a.4.0.	—
do.	16th		Work commenced on new trench.	—
do.	17th		2/Lt Yates rejoins from IV Army School. Lieut A. Grantham rejoins Company from leave to England. Capt. E.W. Smith proceeds to England on leave.	—

WAR DIARY
INTELLIGENCE SUMMARY

(Erase heading not required.)

December 1917.

Army Form C. 2118

Place	Date	Hour	Summary of Events and Information	Remarks and references to Appendices
BOIRY—BECQUERELLE	18th		2nd Lieut. H. Stokes with Sections 1 & 2. relieved Lieut. Jones & Sections 3 & 4. in forward Billets in SHAFT TUNNEL.	a. Rom
do.	20th		The following Officers & N.C.O. were mentioned in despatches by the Field Marshal Commander-in-Chief, of the British Armies in France, for distinguished & gallant service in the field. Vide. London Gazette. 11th December. 1917. Lieut. A. GRANTHAM. R.E. & C.S.M. H. COURT. R.E.	a. Rom
do.	27th		Company was relieved in forward billets by 207th Field Company. R.E. who took over all work in this sector. 2nd Lt. R.F. Stokes, Sections 1 & 2 rejoined Head Quarters at T.P.C. 3.3. on completion of relief. Company under 2nd Lieut. Clark started to proceed to billets at ERVILLERS.	e. Rom 2. Rom
do.	28th		Field Company H.Q. + Section left H.Q. proceed to NOREUIL to take over work from 136th (Yorkshire) Field Coy. R.E. Major G. J. Martin. M.C. R.E. proceeded to R.E. School of Instruction at GHQ and Lieut. A. GRANTHAM. assumes Command of the Company. 2nd Lieut. K. Stokes proceeded on leave to England.	e. Rom e. Rom e. Rom
do.	29th		Company marched to Camp at ERVILLERS in morning. At 4 pm. No 1.2.3 Sections proceeded to advance Billets in NOREUIL to take over all R.E. work in the Right Brigade sector. Transport drew out a No 4 section remained at ERVILLERS. 5. ORE. Reinforcement received.	a. Rom A.G.
ERVILLERS.	30th		Rear section commenced work on store standings of Camp. Forward Sections Normal routine acts.	AG.
do.	31st		" "	A.G.

A. Grantham
2nd Lt.
22nd Field Coy R.E.

Maj. 22nd Field Coy R.E.

Vol 20

Confidential.

War Diary

of

224th Field Company. R.E.

From :-   1st. January 1918.
To :-   31st. January. 1918.

Volume. 20.

WAR DIARY or INTELLIGENCE SUMMARY

Army Form C. 2118

January 1918.

Place	Date	Hour	Summary of Events and Information	Remarks and references to Appendices
ERVILLERS	1st.		Work in NORFUIL sector continued. 3 sections in fire at ERVILLERS. The work in the line consisting of clearing & widening trenches, and erecting 1 dugout work, small elephant shelters. Ground very hard owing to intense frost.	R.9.
			1 O.R. Reinforcement received from R.E. Base Depot. The work of the section at ERVILLERS consisting of erecting Horse Standings for the Battalions of the 120th Inf. Bde., and repairs to accommodation of Brigade. Strength of Company. 7 Officers = 203. O.Rs.	
			Headquarters of Company moved to NORFUIL.	
NORFUIL	2nd.		Work continued as above.	R.9.
do	3rd.		do.	R.9.
do	4th		do	R.9.
do	5th		do	R.9.
do	6th		do. Lieut. Power = No. 4 Section relieved Lt. Clark = No. 2 Sect. at NOREUIL.	R.9.
do	7th		Work as above continued. A slight thaw had commenced & many trenches began to fall in.	R.9.
do	8th		Work continued. Capt. Smith rejoined from leave to U.K. and resumed command of the Company.	R.9.
do	9th		Work continued.	R.9.
do	10th		ditto.	R.9.
do	11th		ditto.	R.9.

Army Form C. 2118

Instructions regarding War Diaries and Intelligence Summaries are contained in F.S. Regs., Part II. and the Staff Manual respectively. Title Pages will be prepared in manuscript.

WAR DIARY
or
INTELLIGENCE SUMMARY
(Erase heading not required.)

January 1918.

Place	Date	Hour	Summary of Events and Information	Remarks and references to Appendices
NOREUIL	12th		The thaw had now set in earnest and the main trenches in this sector were completely blocked in places.	A.9.
do	13th		2/Lt. Fisher rejoined the Company from leave to England. Work continued.	A.9.
do	14th		ditto. 2/Lt. Slack attached to C.R.E.	A.9.
do	15th		ditto. Nearly all infantry working parties had to be concentrated on communication trenches to clear. Advanced room for the prevention of trench falls was started at NOREUIL.	A.9.
do	16th		Work continued. Considerable help had now to be given to Battalions to repair their billets in the lines, as nearly all bivouac billets owing to the thaw had caved in.	A.9.
do	17th		2/Lt. Fisher & No. 2 Section relieved Lieut. Barr. M.C. and No. 1 Section at NOREUIL. Work continued.	A.9.
do	18th		Work continued. At this time 10 deep dugouts in the trenches were being worked. Capt. Smith admitted Hospital. Lieut. Grantham assumed command of the Company. 1 O.R. reinforcement received.	A.9.
do	19th		Work continued.	A.9.
do	20th		do. The completing of new Brigade Headqrs. a new Artillery Group H.Q. at VAULX taken on from an army troop Coy. R.E. 1 O.R. reinforcement received from Base.	A.9.

Army Form C. 2118

WAR DIARY
or
INTELLIGENCE SUMMARY
(Erase heading not required.)

January 1918

Place	Date	Hour	Summary of Events and Information	Remarks and references to Appendices
NOREUIL	21st.		Work continued as before.	R.E.
do	22nd		Work continued as before. A new Battle Line of trenches was started at the rear of NOREUIL and 200 Infantry were supplied every night from the Reserve Battalion of the Brigade.	R.E.
do	23rd		Work continued.	R.E.
do	24th		ditto.	R.E.
do	25th		ditto.	R.E.
do	26th		ditto.	R.E.
do	27th		By this time all communication trenches were deal. Field Forces a No H section were relieved by 1/1 Can. M.C. - No 1. Section at NOREUIL.	R.E.
do	28th		1. O.R. wounded by machine gun fire. Front line. Work continued - slight frost commenced.	R.E.
do	29th		ditto.	R.E.
do	30th		ditto. 2. O.Rs. reinforcements received from R.E. Base Depot.	R.E.
do	31st.		ditto.	R.E.
			Strength of Company. 7 Officers. 201. Other Ranks	

R. Moorhead Lieut R.E.
O/C. 224th Field Company R.E.

WD 21

Confidential

224 Field Co NZE

WAR DIARY

Vol 21.

WAR DIARY
or
INTELLIGENCE SUMMARY

(Erase heading not required.)

February 1918

Army Form C. 2118

Place	Date	Hour	Summary of Events and Information	Remarks and references to Appendices
NOREUIL	1st	—	Work on line continued.	—
—do—	3rd	—	Major E.L. Martin M.C. rejoined Company from leave to England & resumed command of the Company.	—
			169th Field Company R.E. took over work at 120th Inf. Bde. Hd. VAUX.	—
—do—	4th		169th Field Company R.E. takes over work on battle line.	—
—do—	6th		1 Officer of the 169th Field Company R.E. arrived to reconnoitre the sector.	—
—do—	10th		Company relieved in NOREUIL sector by 169th Field Company R.E.	—
			Transport & Hd. Qrs. & 1 section at ERVILLERS moved to new Billets at HAMLINCOURT.	—
			3 Sections billeted & advanced Hd. Qrs moved from NOREUIL to Billets at HAMLINCOURT.	—
HAMLINCOURT	11th			
—do—	12th		I.O.R. Reinforcement from R.E. Base Depot Rouen.	—
—do—	13th		do. do.	—
—do—	14th		do. do.	
—do—	15th			
—do—	16th			
—do—	17th		Lieut. A. Powis & R.E. lst Section proceed to BLAIRVILLE to be attached to 130th Inf. Bde. for purpose of training Infantry in Field Works.	—

WAR DIARY
or
INTELLIGENCE SUMMARY

(Erase heading not required.)

Army Form C. 2118

Place	Date	Hour	Summary of Events and Information	Remarks and references to Appendices
HAMLINCOURT	18th		Company inspected by the C.R.E. 10th Division.	
-do-	26th		H. Qrs. Reinforcements received from R.E. Base Road, Rouen.	
			Lieut. A. Power on N° 14. Section rejoined Company at HAMLINCOURT.	
-do-	27th		Lieut. A.S. Fraser & N°. 3 & 4 Sections moved to N° 43. C.C.S. BOISLEUX-AU-MONT to dismantle C.C.S. under orders of C.E. VII Corps.	
-do-	28th		Headquarters, Mounted Section & N°s 1 & 2 Sections under Major E.A. Mackay M.C. Lieut. L.A. Blaik T.A., H.J. Tooks moved to BULLS at BAILLEULMONT and came under orders of C.E. VI Corps. for purpose of re-erecting	
			N° 43. C.C.S. at LE BAC DU SUD.	

E.A.Mackay
Maj. R.E.
O/C 37th Field Coy Company R.E.

40th Divisional Engineers

WAR DIARY

224th FIELD COMPANY R. E.

MARCH 1 9 1 8

WAR DIARY or INTELLIGENCE SUMMARY

Army Form C. 2118

MARCH 1918.

(Erase heading not required.)

Place	Date	Hour	Summary of Events and Information	Remarks and references to Appendices
BAILLEULMONT	1st		Work on H.3. L.O.S. continued.	
— do —	10th		Lieut. C. Batt. M.C. rejoined company from leave in England.	
— do —	12th		Orders received from H.Q. Division for company to move to No. 6. Camp. HENAECOURT. Capt. A. Grantham. Left in charge of details at BAILLEULMONT.	
HENAECOURT.	12th		Company and transport located at No. 6. Camp. HENAECOURT. Lieut. A. Powis proceeded on leave to U.K.	
— do —	18th		Capt. A. Grantham rejoined company. Lieut. C. Batt. M.C. taking charge of details at BAILLEULMONT.	
HENAECOURT. ARMAGH CAMP HAMELINCOURT. GUEMECOURT.	21st to 25th		The company under Major E.L. Martin M.C. RE. Lieut. G.A. Clarke and Lt. A.K.J. Fisher was engaged in operations from the 21st to the 25th inclusive (see report in annex) Casualties 6 O.R.'s wounded. Including 2 R.O. at duty.	
MONCHY-AU-BOIS	26th		Company moved from MONCHY-AU-BOIS to BIENVILLERS. Dismounted sections engaged in preparing demolitions under orders from CRE. not being at MONCHY-AU-BOIS	
BIENVILLERS.	27th		Company and transport moved to SOMBRIN.	
SOMBRIN.	28th		Company located in billets.	
SEMBRIN.	29th		Company and transport (less a party of 50 men who proceeded by BUS.) moved to ORLENCOURT	
ORLENCOURT.	30th		Mounted portion of company, less Cyclists, marched to TINCQUES, entraining and detraining at NEUF BERQUIN under Lieut. G.A. Clark and Lt. A.K.J. Fisher. The mounted portion moving under Major E.L. Martin. M.C. and Capt. A. Grantham via HOUDAIN, MARLES-Les-MINES, LILLERS to ECQUEDECQUES.	
RUE PROVOST	31st		Dismounted portion of company marched from G.A. Clarke and Lt. A.K.J. Fisher	

WAR DIARY
or
INTELLIGENCE SUMMARY

MARCH 1918.

Place	Date	Hour	Summary of Events and Information	Remarks and references to Appendices
ECQUEA-ECQUES.	3/01.		Marched to FORT ROMPU. Relieving 505th Field Company R.E. in BOIS-GRENIER. Sector. sheet. 36. N.W. 1/20.000	appx
	31st.		Mounted portion of Company under Major Martin. M.C. R.E. and Captain A. Grantham moved thro LILLERS, AUSNES, ROBECQ, MERVILLE, ESTAIRES, to LA BOUARELLE.	appx
				appx

R L Martin Major R.E.
O/C. 505th Field Company. R.E.

At 8 a.m. the 21st March 1918 the Company was in
No. 6 Camp, BEND COURT.

Orders were received by wire from "G" 40th Division
ordering Company to move at once to ARMAGH CAMP, HAMELENCOURT.

The Company arrived at 11 p.m.

Orders were received from the C.R.E. for the Company
to hold a portion of the Army Line, from 300 yards north of the
COJUEL RIVER to S.23.b.9.6. (Sheet 51b.S.W. 1/20,000), at 4 a.m.
22nd March 1918. Having on the right flank the 12th (S) Battn.
Yorkshire Regt. (Pioneers). Left flank not held. This was held
until 6 a.m. 23rd March, 1918, when the Company was relieved in
this line by a Company of the 2nd Battn. Coldstream Guards.

Orders were received 2 hours later to move to GOMIECOURT.

The Company was then ordered to hold the line from
B.25.b.4.4. to H.1.b.5.7. Sheet 57c. N.W. 1/20,000.

The left flank being held by one Company of the 12th (S)
Battn. Yorkshire Regt. (Pioneers). Right flank not held but
protected by posts in front of BEHAGNIES. Nothing of interest
occured on this date.

On the night of the 24th March 1918 it was reported,
at 8 p.m., that the enemy had broken through on the left flank.

This seemed to be supported by the barrage fire opened
by the Artillery. Detachments of the 58th Machine Gun Battn.
reported in the trenches. I ordered them to take up a position on
my left flank at B.25.b.8.5. Sheet 57c. N.W. 1/20,000, so as to
bring approaching and flanking fire and secure my flank.

The Company of Pioneers established communication with
a Battalion of the 59th Division holding a trench on the eastern
side of the ERVILLERS ROAD.

The Company stood to till dawn, no sign of the enemy was
seen although the barrage continued and the trenches came under
hostile shell fire.

On the morning of the 25th March, 1918, at an S.O.S.
signal the Company stood to at 5-30 a.m. Enemy were seen on the
Eastern side of the ERVILLERS - BEHAGNIES Road. On the left flank
our troops were seen to be retiring, but shortly afterwards the enemy
were driven back by the Artillery, and Machine Gun fire from the
posts established on my left flank.

At 7-0 a.m. A & B Companies of the 20th Battn. Middlesex
Regt. reported in the trench. I arranged with the O.C. for them to
hold a disused trench in front of BEHAGNIES some 50 yards ------

(2).

--- some 50 yards, in front of my trench.

They reported they had been compelled to withdraw from a position south of MORY owing to the troops having retired on both flanks.

I got information sent from Brigade Headquarters that the enemy attack was developing on my right flank and all possible measures were to be taken to hold it up. I therefore altered the positions of my machine guns to cover the threatened flank.

At 10 a.m. O.C. 20th Battn. Middlesex Regt. visited the position and approved of the dispositions of defence, and stated that he would assume command from then onwards. His second in command he left in the forward trench, and established his Battalion Head Quarters in the sunken road in rear of the position.

At 2 p.m. many troops were seen retiring, and those that came in the immediate vicinity of my trench were ordered to remain. The trenches during this time were continuously shelled with Field and Heavy Artillery. BEHAGNIES receiving much attention.

At 2-30 p.m. signs of a general retirement on all sides was very evident, our Artillery putting down a defensive barrage behind BEHAGNIES, this caused casualties in my trench. I got into touch with the Forward Observation Officer who had received information that the enemy were occupying BEHAGNIES. I established the fact that this was not so, and the range was accordingly lengthened.

At 3 p.m. continuous parties of our troops were retiring and information was received from the O.C. 14th Battn. Argyll & Sutherland Regt. that our right flank had been driven in and a general retirement ordered.

I consulted Major Hill, 20th Battn. Middlesex Regt. and we decided our position was to be held until written orders were received from higher authority ordering our withdrawal.

At 4 p.m. the enemy was seen approaching from the S of BEHAGNIES and succeeded in establishing a Machine gun position at H.1.c.4.7. Enemy artillery became very active.

Troops were then seen debouching from MORY and the ridge E of BEHAGNIES, both parties converging on my left flank.

(3).

They were prevented from approaching within 300 yards of the ERVILLERS - BEHAGNIES Road by our machine gun and rifle fire.

Large bodies of troops were seen retiring on the left flank. I went at once to the threatened point and found that the Machine gunners had withdrawn and my left flank was thoroughly exposed. I therefore ordered B. Company of the 20th Battn. Middlesex Regt. to withdraw from the front line trench and man a series of posts running from ELM WOOD to E.25.c.6.9. to B.25.c.9.7., which had been previously dug to support this point.

Twenty minutes later the enemy appeared in large force, headed by a mounted Officer, who was instantly shot by Lieut. G.A. Clark, R.E., causing the enemy to waver. Rapid fire was opened and the enemy driven back. Parties of our troops were seen moving forward and occupied a line on my immediate left flank, connection was at once established with them.

From now onwards the enemy made repeated attempts to advance but was unsuccessful.

At 7 p.m., under cover of darkness and a rainstorm, the enemy attempted to rush my line of posts on the left flank.

After twenty minutes heavy fighting he was driven off.

At 10 p.m. it was discovered that the troops on our left flank had retired to a position in rear, of my then defensive line.

The O.C. 20th Battn. Middlesex Regt. came to the trench and the situation was discussed. He stated that it was decided with the O.C's. Battalions in that line that no good purpose would be served by holding the present line if certain posts in front were established to control the valley.

O.C. 20th Battn. Middlesex Regt. went with me to select posts for these positions, and arranged with me to cover the withdrawal of his Companies to new posts and then to withdraw my men.

During the withdrawal of the two Companies, which was rendered very difficult owing to clearness of visibility due to full moon, the enemy again attempted to rush the line of posts, which were now held by this Company but was driven off having suffered casualties and my Company was successfully withdrawn.

27/3/18.

G.R. Martin Major. R.E.
O/Commanding 224th Field Company. R.E.

40th Divisional Engineers.

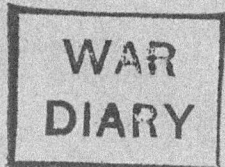

224th FIELD COMPANY R. E.

APRIL 1918

SECRET

Vol 22

War Diary.
(Vol. 23.)
April 1918.
(1st – 30th)

224 Field Coy. R.E.

Vol 23

Army Form C. 2118.

WAR DIARY
or
INTELLIGENCE SUMMARY.
(Erase heading not required.)

APRIL 1918.

Place	Date	Hour	Summary of Events and Information	Remarks and references to Appendices
FORT ROMPU H.7.d. (Sheet 36)	1st.		Company employed on line and back area work. Taken over from 505" Field Coy R.E. Work includes a reinforced concrete Brigade H.Q. at BARTLETT FARM (H.26.a.4.3)	A/4
	2nd.		Work on line continued. Maintenance of bridges (pontoon) for use in emergency across the River LYS had also been taken over from 505 Field Coy R.E. also the testing of the explosive etc. for blowing up of the main swing bridge at BAC-ST-MAUR. Four more emergency cork raft bridges over the River LYS started.	A/4
	3rd.		Work continued	A/4
	4th.			A/4
	5th.			A/4
	6th.		(Effective Strength 6 Off. 197 O.R.)	A/4
	7th.			
	8th.		The four cork raft bridges completed. M.C. proceeded to C.C.S. (Sick) Command of company taken over meantime by Capt. A. Grantham R.E. Lieut W. Price R.E. returned from leave.	A/4
	9th.		Enemy attacked. Company engaged in active operations	
	4 am.		On 4 a.m. the enemy started an intense bombardment of the trenches of our sector and the accompanying shell continued at 5.0 a.m.	
	5 a.		at which hour I moved the company and others to Slaves to "battle order." Thereminder the field off for bridge investigation. The party which had been Company to be nearby to move at once.	
	6.10 a.		Orders throughout the company received from C.R.E. Bridges arrived by 6.15 a.m. Only three sections of the company were at my disposal, 2/Lieut K.J. Fidel and no section being away in the trenches with the 20th Middlesex Regt, taking part on a minor operation.	

WAR DIARY or INTELLIGENCE SUMMARY

Army Form C. 2118.

APRIL 1918.

Place	Date	Hour	Summary of Events and Information	Remarks and references to Appendices
	9th (cont)	Noon.	Bridges were all guarded and patrols watched all approaches and kept a small reserve at Coy. H.Q., FORT ROMPU. It was evident that the enemy was not far away and received news that he was in FLEUR BAIX. My transport was man-handled to the opposite side of the road at once & horses came and took it to the horse-lines. Two double limbers (G.S.) were destroyed by shell fire. Orders to horselines were sent direct by C.R.E. for all transport to move to DOULIEU area.	
		1.30 p.m.	The enemy was very near & machine gun fire swept some parts of the ground.	
		2.15 p.m.	The main swing bridge at BAC ST MAUR was destroyed. This bridge had been ready charged all for some 40 days. The leads from the exploder to the charges had to be renewed three times by Lieut CLARK, M.C. and Sergt TERRIOS R.E. The platoon and Cork bridge were destroyed (all under M.G. fire) as soon as all the infantry and guns had crossed; The last C.O.R. bridge near the Brewery FORT ROMPU being destroyed at 2.30 p.m.	
		2.30 p.m.	The enemy seemed now to have established Machine guns in trees at BAC ST MAUR which enfiladed the whole of the river. The company now men back & concentrated and held & times in M.T.C. (sheet 36) with whole of the 40th Div M.G. Battn, now right flank of H 120th Inf Bde (Royal Scots Fusiliers) on our left.	
		3.45 p.m.	It was evident that the enemy had covered through at BAC ST MAUR and was advancing up the CROIX DU BAC Road. Our right flank had therefore to give way. The right flank seemed to be badly broken and remnants were collected to hold in G.6.d.	

WAR DIARY or INTELLIGENCE SUMMARY

Army Form C. 2118.

APRIL 1918.

Place	Date	Hour	Summary of Events and Information	Remarks and references to Appendices
	9th (Cont)	6.30 p.m.	A Brigade of the 25th Divn. came up into the line and we operated with them, still holding to the line.	
NEUF BERQUIN	10th	2.0 a.m.	This Brigade sent forward and counter attacked at CROIX DU BAC, we being in support.	
		6.30 a.m.	Some orders were came into support and relieved my company, 2/Provost forward towards DOULIEU, and on my way received orders that all the companies (of 40th Divl R.E.) should concentrate at the horse lines at RUE PROVOST near NEUF BERQUIN. 2/Lieut Parker and 1/Corp Sapper who had been detached for work in the line, also rejoined at horse lines.	
MERRIS		3.0 p.m.	Warning orders received for the Three Field Coys to support the 119th Inf Bde. if required, but for the time being to remain at Transport lines. Transport lines were back to MERRIS (Lieut. C. Carr M.C. and Nissen at Transport lines here in the 11th (Bn.)	
LA VERRIER		5.0 p.m.	Warning order cancelled and the Company proceeded to LA VERRIER under order of G.O.C. 119th Inf Bde. to defend LA VERRIER, on arriving to the situation forward the Companies were attached to the front line to fill the gap existing between the 83rd Bde. (29th Division) and the Royal North Lancs. (operating with 125th Inf. Bde.) on the right. We took position the field corp. line from A.15.b. to crossroads in A.22.a. The 229th Infantry was on the left, 224th (Sheet 36) field cap in the centre, and 231st field cap on the right.	
	11th		Touch could not be obtained during darkness with the people on our left, but it was soon apparent at Battalion of York & Lancs. was found on our left operating under order of 88th Inf Bde. This line we held throughout the morning until 11 a.m. when our right flank being driven in a withdrawal of Throughout becoming necessary, pivoting on the left flank. to LE PETIT MORTIER being taken by the enemy, and the	

WAR DIARY or INTELLIGENCE SUMMARY

Army Form C. 2118.

April 1918.

Place	Date	Hour	Summary of Events and Information	Remarks and references to Appendices
LA VERRIER	11th (Cont.)		Though flank of the 231st and 34th G.R.2 was still the LA VERRIER – STEENWERCK road.	
		2.30pm	Touch was lost with the right flank of the YORK & LANCS Batt.	
		4.00pm	Enfilade fire made further withdrawals necessary until a line was formed again near MAISON BLANCHE at 6.15 pm. During the withdrawal several casualties were inflicted. This line was held in force and patrols were pushed forward towards LA BECQUE FARM to obtain touch with the enemy.	
		6.30pm	Orders received from O.C. 25th Battn, 25th Division, that 31st Divn was about to counter-attack and the field companies and 25th Divl. details were ordered to form a defensive flank on the left – the left resting on MAISON BLANCHE & the right on CORPSE IN A.13.d. Here rifle posts were established. The 31st Divn. counter-attacked from the right and came in front of the line held by us. At 11 pm we were relieved by the DURHAM LIGHT INFANTRY. On relief the field companies concentrated and marched to BAILLEUL, where they halted 2 hours, and then moved to hutted area between STRAZEELE & PRADEELE.	
STRAZEELE	12th	2 pm	Orders received to prepare for the defence of STRAZEELE; picks taking use of tools. Digging parties arranged from composite battalions of 119th & 121st Inf. Bde.	
HONDEGHEM	13th		The work proceeded during the night. The following morning (13th) orders were received to withdraw all field companies to HONDEGHEM, & march from there to back areas to re-fit. (Effective strength 5 Off. 166 O.R.)	
CORMETTE	14th	6.0 pm	Company arrived at CORMETTE (Near ST OMER) at 6.0 pm. All men billetted in barns. Head Quarters at the CHATEAU.	

WAR DIARY or INTELLIGENCE SUMMARY

Army Form C. 2118.

APRIL 1918

Place	Date	Hour	Summary of Events and Information	Remarks and references to Appendices
CORMETTE	15th		Company commenced to refit. All equipment was checked and deficiencies indented for.	J.G.
	16th		The company (with the other two field companies of the Division) was inspected by the CRE, 40th Division.	P.G.
	17th		Refitting and training continued.	P.G.
	18th		Warning orders received that 224th Field Coy R.E. would form part of the Composite Bde. and must be brought to establishment strength in men and equipment. Sappers and drivers to do this were attached from 229th Field Coy. Horses and also complete limbers were also attached from 229th Field Coy. The 40th Bde Field Coys were inspected by the G.O.C. 40th Div., who congratulated all ranks on their behaviour in the recent operations.	P.G.
	19th		Others received that Composite Brigade was ordered 4 hours notice to move.	P.G.
	20th		Orders received that company would move forward again on 21st. For opened work with Composite Brigade under VIII Corps. (Effective strength 5 Off. 174 OR)	P.G.
ZUITPEENE	21st		Company moved to new ZUITPEENE (O.13.a – Sheet 27). Billeted in tents.	P.G.
HARDIFORT J.25.d.3.8. (Sheet 27)	22nd		Coy moved to HARDIFORT. Billets in barns and tents. O.C. had moved new Corps line to having by Composite Brigade with CRE, 140th Bde & G.O.C. Composite Bde.	P.G.
	23rd		Work started on new line. The sector the company authorised being from Nol OUDEZEELE to BRUSSEL HOOCH. South Battalion supplied half their strength for working parties. Line was constructed of posts 20 feet long (behind hedges, where possible) at intervals of 30 feet. Ground in most cases was wet in consequence of which, 6 breastworks had to be made through the Composite Brigade threshed out at the Battalion.	P.G.
	24th		Work continued.	P.G.

Army Form C. 2118.

WAR DIARY
or
INTELLIGENCE SUMMARY.
(Erase heading not required.)

APRIL 1918

Place	Date	Hour	Summary of Events and Information	Remarks and references to Appendices
HONDTFORT	25th		Work continued.	A.4.
	26th		" "	A.4.
	27th		" " (Effective Strength 27th, 5 Off., 174 O.R.) Working parties of the Coolies Brigade were recalled from work at noon to hold themselves in readiness to move to another area. New line behind post line – MAIN LINE OF RESISTANCE – marked out by C.R.E. 40 Div.	A.4.
	28th		Instruction received that Chinese white labour Companies would constitute the working parties. Coolies Brigade moved from the area to PROVEN. Order received that the Southern half of the out-posts from BRUSSCH HOEK to STEENVOORDE ROAD to CHINESE WHITE Labour were now to be taken over. Sappers set looking No Chinese Labour yet available for work out post. Line of Resistance, and finishing off posts in line.	A.4.
	29th		On Chinese Labour Cny. 450 working strength: started work on line of Resistance, on TROIS ROIS in S.8 sub-sector – used as white labour by employed with starting at the northern boundary of the (Sheet 27) and working southwards on out-post line connecting southern.	A.4.
	30th			

Marantham Major RE
OC 224 Field CoRE

CONFIDENTIAL

WAR DIARY

OF

224 FIELD COMPANY, R.E.

May 1st 1918 to May 31st 1918

Volume 23.

Army Form C. 2118.

WAR DIARY
or
INTELLIGENCE SUMMARY
(Erase heading not required.)

MAY 1918.

Place	Date	Hour	Summary of Events and Information	Remarks and references to Appendices
HARDIFORT J.25.b.3.8 (Sheet 27 - Belgium & part of France)	1st		Work continued on the WINNEZEELE line. Observation line, originally connecting strong points, being made into a continuous line of trenches. Line of resistance also continued. 1 Chinese Labour Coy. and 3 White labour coys. supplied the working parties.	A.Y.
	2nd		Work continued	A.Y.
	3rd		"	A.Y.
	4th		Military Medal awarded to A/Sgt Scrivin & for gallantry in the field during operations between March 21st and 26th. Effective strength 5 Off. 174 O.R.	A.Y.
	5th		Work continued. 20 O.R. returned to 229 Area G.P.E.	A.Y.
	6th		" 2 New Kent R.E. and 9 O.R. joined Coy. from France	A.Y.
	7th		The southern part of the subsection from BRUSSEL HOOGH to STEENVOORDE ROAD was taken over again from the French.	A.Y.
	8th		Work continued	A.Y.
	9th		2nd Lieut Juleff joined company from Base.	A.Y.
	10th		Work continued	A.Y.
	11th		" Effective strength 7 Off. 182 O.R.	A.Y.

Army Form C. 2118.

WAR DIARY
or
INTELLIGENCE SUMMARY.
(Erase heading not required.)

Instructions regarding War Diaries and Intelligence Summaries are contained in F.S. Regs., Part II. and the Staff Manual respectively. Title pages will be prepared in manuscript.

MAY. 1918.

Place	Date	Hour	Summary of Events and Information	Remarks and references to Appendices
HARDIFORT	12th.		Work as before.	A.9.
	13th.		Lieut. G. Clark R.E. proceeded to England on special leave.	A.9.
	14th.		C.R.E. held conference with all the Field Company Commanders. O.C. Company & C.R.E. went round lines of trenches with G.O.C. 40th Div., and Maj. Gen. P. Kenyon R.E. Borhams slightly altered, the line of trenches being taken in front of RYVELD and OUDEZEELE.	A.9.
	15th.		Enemy active at night, dropping bombs on the enemy. Work continued.	A.9.
	16th.		Lieut. Clark R.E. awarded M.C. for gallantry in the field during operations Mar 21st to 28th, on the SOMME.	A.9.
	17th.			A.9.
	18th.		M.Sergt Terris awarded the 6 M.M. C.H. Carp. and Pioneer Harrison awarded M.M., all for gallantry in the field in operations between 9th and 13th April during the Battle of the Lys.	A.9.
	19th.		Effective Strength 7 Offr. 182 O.R.	A.9.
	20th.		Work continued	A.9.
	21st.		O.C. went round Keep Resistance with C.R.E. working on the Support line.	A.9.

Army Form C. 2118.

WAR DIARY
or
INTELLIGENCE SUMMARY.
(Erase heading not required.)

Instructions regarding War Diaries and Intelligence Summaries are contained in F. S. Regs., Part II and the Staff Manual respectively. Title pages will be prepared in manuscript.

Place	Date	Hour	Summary of Events and Information	Remarks and references to Appendices
	22nd		Work continued.	
	23rd		do.	
	24th		Major Master M.C. R.E. returned from sick-leave and took over Command of the Company.	2mm
	25th		Effective Strength 7 Offs and 184 O.R.	3mm
	26th		C.R.E's conference with Field Company Commanders	2mm
	30th		Lieut Godden M.C. R.E. returns from leave.	
	31st		Effective Strength 7 Offs and 185 O.R.	2mms

Approved
Mastin
O.C. 221 Field Company R.E.

CONFIDENTIAL.

WAR DIARY

of

224 FIELD COMPANY, R.E.

JUNE 1st 1918 – JUNE 30th 1918.

VOLUME 25.

Army Form C. 2118.

WAR DIARY
~~INTELLIGENCE SUMMARY.~~
(Erase heading not required.)

JUNE 1918

Instructions regarding War Diaries and Intelligence Summaries are contained in F. S. Regs., Part II. and the Staff Manual respectively. Title pages will be prepared in manuscript.

Place	Date	Hour	Summary of Events and Information	Remarks and references to Appendices
HARDIFORT	1st		Captain A. Grantham proceeded on leave. Effective Strength 7 Offs 185 OR	e.2000
T.25,6.3,8. (Sheet 27)	3rd		Company Hdrs Guide and No 1 and 2 sections moved to B ALEMBERG.	e.2000
			No 3 section under Lieut Powel R.E., remained incomplete at work with WINNEZEELE line.	e.2000
BALEMBERG H.33, 6.5, 6. (Sheet 27)	4th		Major Weir and Lt Brember reported. Effective Strength (8 Offs) 7 Offs 182 OR	e.2000
	8th		Lieut Clark and No 3 section rejoined the Company having finished approval work.	e.2000
	9th		Area 1 to 187 (Chinese) Labour Company.	
			Lieut Powel and No 4 section reported to the 251st Coy Company and transferred	e.2000
	10th		now stationed at BALEMBERG.	
	12th		Due to attacks to East field Company R.E. for work under the Corps	e.2000
			Sapph Officer, VII Corps. 7 Offs 182 OR	e.2000
			Effective Strength	e.2000
	15th		H.R.E.B.T.O 4 K defences with a view to the Company being called upon to	
			attend this d.o.e	
	16th		O.C. accompanied G.O.C. 151 Inf Bde in reconnaissance of the West	
			Lieut Powel had m/s the WINNEZEELE line to the O.P.S with C.R.A., VII Corps R.A.	e.2000
			Lieut Col. R.P. Pakenham Walsh MC, RE, calls at the Camp in accompany the	e.2000
			duties of CRE 41st Division	a.2000

Army Form C. 2118.

WAR DIARY
or
INTELLIGENCE SUMMARY.
(Erase heading not required.)

Instructions regarding War Diaries and Intelligence Summaries are contained in F. S. Regs., Part II. and the Staff Manual respectively. Title pages will be prepared in manuscript.

Place	Date	Hour	Summary of Events and Information	Remarks and references to Appendices
BALEMBERG	22.		Received orders from CRE. The proposed move to W. HAZEBROUCK line. Strength 7 Off 162 OR	
	23		The company moved to U.18.d. central, dismounted men by lorry, mounted men by march route.	
WALLON CAPPELL U.18.d.S.S.	25th		1 Officer and 9 OR remained behind to hand over, 2/Lieut Jukoff RE and 9 OR rejoined	
	27th		Practice concentration. The Company moved to U.19.d. as would happen in case of an enemy attack. Cpl. Grantham proceeded to T.10.d. The horse-lines in that eventuality. Pte. I.J. O'Connor CR. was attached to the Company in the 11th left for Egypt.	
	29th		Effective Strength 7 Off. 167 OR. The Company in the area so employed in wiring, clearing the fields of fire, and generally improving the W. HAZEBROUCK line, and providing artillery observation posts.	
	30th		The CRE inspects the Company.	

Myor RE
OC 2nd Irish O RE

CONFIDENTIAL.

WAR DIARY

of

224 FIELD COMPANY, R.E.

From 1st July 1918.
To 31st July 1918.

Volume 26.

224TH FIELD COMPANY, R.E.
No.
Date 31-7-18

WAR DIARY or INTELLIGENCE SUMMARY.

Army Form C. 2118.

JULY 1918.

Place	Date	Hour	Summary of Events and Information	Remarks and references to Appendices
WALLON CAPPEL (M 18 d 55) Sheet 27	1st		The Company still employed on improving the West HAZEBROUCK Line, wiring and erecting splinter-proof OP's. Yprès Poles procured in lieu.	—
	6th		Effective strength 7 Off. 166 OR.	—
			2nd Lt. D. Haychuck Rue continued.	—
EECKE Q 25 d 9·9 Sheet 27	11th		Company hand to & from near EECKE and now come under the orders of Major Bellamy, CRE, Le PEUPLIER Switch. Company employed on construction and improvement of LE PEUPLIER SWITCH, in continuation of 7th W. HAZEBROUCK line. Company hand Constitute Reserve to "Bellamys" force in case of enemy attack. (i.e. troops commanded by Major C. Bellamy DSO RE, CRE Le Peuplier Switch, as per XIII Corps Order.)	—
	12		19 OR joined Coy from Base.	—
	13.		Effective Strength 7 Off 164 OR.	—
	15		4 Off + 100 OR moved to Battle Position for test Mobilization on receipt of orders. Stand To's under OC Coy (Major Markin, Res Club, reported on recpt of call)	again
	16th		2/Lieut K.S. Drake RE rejoined company from leave.	again
	20th		Effective Strength 7 Officers 180 OR.	—

Army Form C. 2118.

WAR DIARY
or
INTELLIGENCE SUMMARY.
(Erase heading not required.)

July 1918.

Place	Date	Hour	Summary of Events and Information	Remarks and references to Appendices
EECKE	26th		4 O.R. joined company from Base.	nem
Q.25.d.9.9.	27th		13 O.R. joined company from Base	nem
(Sheet 27)	31st		Effective Strength 4 off. 201 O.R.	nem

A.E.Maskew
Major R.E.
O.C. 224 Field Company R.E.

— CONFIDENTIAL —

WAR DIARY

224th FIELD COMPANY. R.E.

FROM

AUGUST 1st 1918 To AUGUST 31st 1918.

VOLUME 27

WAR DIARY
or
INTELLIGENCE SUMMARY.

Army Form C. 2118.

AUGUST 1918.

(Erase heading not required.)

Place	Date	Hour	Summary of Events and Information	Remarks and references to Appendices
EECKE. Q 25 d. 9.9. Sheet 27.	1st		Company employed improving "B" line (a line of trenches in continuation of LE PEUPLIER Switch). The work chiefly consists of revetting the firestep and	app.
			building dug-outs and battalion Head Quarters. Three huts were also built	app.
			with splinter proof covers	app.
	3rd		Effective strength of company 4 offs. 200 O.R.	app.
	4th		Work continued. The weather of this period was exceptionally fine, and so	app.
	5th		-do-	app.
	6th		-do-	app.
	7th		-do-	app.
	8th		-do-	app.
	9th		-do- Major F.L. Martin M.C. O.C. No 9 Coy LE PEUPLIER SWITCH Lieutenant Colonel of Commander	app.
	10th		Aircraft of Company 4 offs. 201 O.R.	app.
	11th		The work being carried on in dumbings, a medical Inspection of the whole Coy.	app.
			was carried out the M.O. reporting that the condition and health of the men	app.
			of Coy. was satisfactory first	app.
	12th		The section of "B" line finished and no section was moved	app.
			to a new section extending from to trunk mining system	app.

Army Form C. 2118.

WAR DIARY
or
INTELLIGENCE SUMMARY.
(Erase heading not required.)

AUGUST 1918. *continued*

Instructions regarding War Diaries and Intelligence Summaries are contained in F. S. Regs., Part II. and the Staff Manual respectively. Title pages will be prepared in manuscript.

Place	Date	Hour	Summary of Events and Information	Remarks and references to Appendices
EECKE Q.25.d.9.9.	13th		Work continued as usual	
	14"		"	
Sheet 27	15th			
	16"			
	17"			
	18"			
	19"			
	20"			
	21st		Warning order received that 40th Division would take over the VIEUX BERQUIN Sector from the 31st Division, and that 2nd S.C.Coy would take over from 211th Field A.E. Orders received that no extra work was to be done on "B" line by this unit.	
	22nd		Major E.L. Maclin M.C. R.E. relieved & took over the Coy, and went round the sector to be taken over with the O.C. 211th Fd.Coy.R.E. Work in "B" line handed over to 235 A.T.C. R.E.	
	23rd		All sections officers went round the new sector with officers of 211 Field Coy R.E.	
HAZEBROUCK GARAGE D.5.c.9.1 Sheet 36 A	24th		Company moved by echelon took over all Demolition work.	
	25th		Company employed in clearing and making up forward roads, erecting and camouflaging bridge in camp, 8 Coys at 36A/E.11.c.3.1, putting in telephone shelter for Brigade H.Q at E.15.c.65.60 (Sheet 36 A)	
			MOLEGHEM FARM (E.10.c) and establishing advanced R.E. H.Q at E.15.c.65.60 (Sheet 36 A)	
	26		Work as before continued	
SANITAS CORNER E.15.c.65.60	27		2 Sections of Coy H.Q moved up to SANITAS CORNER 2 Sect transported to HAZEBROUCK GARAGE Work continued	
	28		One more section moved to SANITAS CORNER. The following officers are now at SANITAS	
	29		Maj Maclin, Lieut Poussaint, Church, Todhin, Dicker	

Army Form C. 2118.

WAR DIARY
or
INTELLIGENCE SUMMARY.
(Erase heading not required.)

AUGUST 1918 continued.

Place	Date	Hour	Summary of Events and Information	Remarks and references to Appendices
SANITAS CORNER			Armoury Lorries kept Hdqt field Coy frames in Crossroads E.19.b.8.8.	
			E.24.Cel.Gd. — F.21.Cel.Gd. (independent of Battalion Boundaries.)	
	30th		Northern Boundary of 4th side of (Day to Coy) with the HAZEBROUCK - BAILLEUL Ry.	
			Work Continued.	
	31st		Company proceeded to clean road from 17.13.a.6.3 to F.14.d.3.4. and repair bomb holes	
			to Hdqt. destroyed by enemy to allow trips to follow up his retirement	
			(sheet 36 1" NE)	
			200 Infantry from 121st Inf Bde. were attached for purpose of assisting to	
			clear roads.	

J R Martin Major RE
OC 2nd Field Company RE

CONFIDENTIAL

War Diary

of

224 Field Company, R.E.

From:- 1st Sept. 1918.

To:- 30th Sept. 1918.

Volume 28.

Army Form C. 2118.

WAR DIARY
or
INTELLIGENCE SUMMARY.
(Erase heading not required.)

SEPTEMBER 1918.

Instructions regarding War Diaries and Intelligence Summaries are contained in F. S. Regs., Part II. and the Staff Manual respectively. Title pages will be prepared in manuscript.

Place	Date	Hour	Summary of Events and Information	Remarks and references to Appendices
SANITAS CORNER E.15.C 65.b/30A	1st		The Company was employed in clearing roads and filling shell holes and bridge at F.14.9.3.3	
	2nd		Work on roads and bridge continued. Shot sections moved to F.17.a.2.8.	
	3rd		-ditto- No 2 section moved to F.17.a.2.8.	
NOOTE BOOM, A/F.17.a.2.8	4th		-ditto- H.Q. & transport moved to F.17.a.2.8.	
	5th		Company employed in constructing in bridge and the STEENBECQUE to take 3 Tons and on forward roads. Officer O.C. had proceeds to RETS Region for another Rifle Corps of Instruction.	
	6th		Took to above continued.	
	7th		-ditto- Officers strength 7 officers and 206 OR	
	8th		-ditto-	
A/A 18 d 3.3	9th		The front sections moved forward to F 36/A 18. d 3.3 ? east of STEENWERCK. H.Q. established in a cottage at A.14.H.3.3. Bridge over STEENBECQUE on	
	10th		STEENWERK Main Road (A.14.C.65.30) commenced to take all traffic. Transport moved to A.D.a Central (A.a. 36) - new number columns	
	11th		Work on roads and bridge continued. 1 OR wounded (Shell fire) in his tent, during a heavy concentration on an adjacent battery position.	
	12th		1 OR killed (Shell fire) whilst at work on forward roads	
	13th		Work started by no section on the NIEPPE System. The 40th Division (coming) been ordered to hold this section of this system as a defensive line. the CRE advised GOC Division to establish a series of posts there was	

Army Form C. 2118.

WAR DIARY
or
INTELLIGENCE SUMMARY.
(Erase heading not required.)

SEPTEMBER 1918.

Instructions regarding War Diaries and Intelligence Summaries are contained in F.S. Regs., Part II. and the Staff Manual respectively. Title pages will be prepared in manuscript.

Place	Date	Hour	Summary of Events and Information	Remarks and references to Appendices
A.16.A.33.	13th cont		agreed to and the following 8 posts were attacked and taken as ordered. No 1. B.16.d.95.60; No 2. B.16.d.45.00; No 3. B.22.b.50.60; No 4. B.22.d.80.95; No 5. B.22.d.40.45; No 6. B.28.b.35.40; No 7. B.28.d.50.50; No 8. H.3.b.60.55; (See 36 NW)	2 Run
	14th		Officers strength 7 Officers 1.198 OR. The company advanced responsibly for all work in the Divisional Sector of the NIEPPE System, being relieved of work in order by 229 Field Company R.E.	2 Run
	15th		2 OR. wounded in billets, work in posts continued.	2 Run
	16th		1 OR wounded (Machine gun fire) while at work on bridge near PT. WARNAVE Pt. at B.23.a.1.9. Barrel piers constructed W.1.B. in anticipation of crossing the LYS.	2 Run
	16th		Extract from London Gazette 24/01 16-1918. T/Lieut. Garrett RE (awarded M.C. for the following) "This officer displayed admirable courage and resource during repeated enemy attacks. He went forward constantly to a village in front of our line and brought back valuable information as to the position	2 Run

Army Form C. 2118.

WAR DIARY
or
INTELLIGENCE SUMMARY.
(Erase heading not required.)

SEPTEMBER 1918

Instructions regarding War Diaries and Intelligence Summaries are contained in F.S. Regs., Part II. and the Staff Manual respectively. Title pages will be prepared in manuscript.

Place	Date	Hour	Summary of Events and Information	Remarks and references to Appendices
A.18.d.3.3	16th Cont.		of the enemy and of a machine gun later on controlling the fire of the Engineers and Infantry in the trenches, he drove back the enemy and checked the general advance for a time. He showed a complete disregard for his own safety."	
	17th		Work on posts and barbed wire continued	app.
	18th		ditto	app.
	19th		ditto	app.
	20th		Capt. A. Lewishan granted leave to Paris from 21st to 28th Sept. 1918.	app.
	21st		Work on posts continued. Lifter Lt. Joseph Jefferson sent 19th IB	app.
	22nd		ditto	
	23rd		ditto	
	24th		2/Lieut W. Power, 23rd Cheshire Regt. attached 22nd Field Company R.E. proceeded to Hospital (sick)	app.
	25th		CRE inspected work in the line with the O.C. While at work men on fatigue duty Civilians are occasionally fired on by m.g. fire Infantry during night 25/26.	app.
	26"		Work on posts continued	app.

Army Form C. 2118.

WAR DIARY or INTELLIGENCE SUMMARY.

(Erase heading not required.)

SEPTEMBER 1918

Place	Date	Hour	Summary of Events and Information	Remarks and references to Appendices
36/A.16.d.3.3.	27th		The Corps Commander decided that it was necessary to screen the NIEPPE SYSTEM. All other work was ordered to cease, pending the completion of this screening. During the night of 27/28th, material was collected and carried to the cane & work. Horse driven holes dug and poles laid in for 700 yards of screening front.	8 km
	28th		Camouflage carried out, framework and wires& ready for lowering. Effective aircraft 4 Officers and 201 O.R.	9 km 20 km
	29th		On return from work on early morning of 28th, 5 O.R. of the Company and 1 O.R. of 23rd Cheshire attached the Company were wounded by shell fire, from F.K.Hin of the Company died of wounds during the morning. O.C. made a reconnaissance of the NIEPPE SYSTEM together with the G.O.C. 121 Bde. and found the position of our huts in confluence with orders of G.O.C. XV Corps.	8 km 8 km 8 km
	30th		700 yards of screening successfully erected in night of 29th. New Advert R.E. granted leave to U.K. from 30.9/18. to 14.10/18. O.C. made a reconnaissance of the R. LYS from H.1.d.7.0. to H.3.d.9.5. (See 36 NW) for purpose of finding positions for temporary bridges for passage of Infantry, pending the approval of the C.R.E.	8 km

R Wynter Major R.E.
O.C. 224 Field Company R.E.

CONFIDENTIAL

WAR DIARY

OF

224 FIELD COMPANY, R.E.

From:- 1st Oct. 1918.
To:- 31st Oct. 1918.

VOLUME 29.

Army Form C. 2118.

WAR DIARY
or
INTELLIGENCE SUMMARY.
(Erase heading not required.)

OCTOBER 1918.

Place	Date	Hour	Summary of Events and Information	Remarks and references to Appendices
A.18.d.3.3 (Sheet 36.) In STEENWERCK	1st		Company employed in clearing the main road to PONT DE NIEPPE and collecting material for bridging the R. WARNAVE. The ponteens and horses attend to at 14:00 of R.E. readiness to cross the R. LYS	2.um
	2nd		O.R.E and O.C. have a reconnaissance of the R. LYS between H.3.b.5.9.9 & 3.d.4.5. and crossed to the opposite bank and established connection with patrols of the 61st Div. It was decided at noon to throw a pontoon bridge across the river at H.3.c.6.7 (36). This bridge was completed at 15.15 hrs. A barrel pier bridge was also commenced at H.3.d.5.4 and completed at 19.00. O.C. reconnaissance of the road from BAC ST MAUR to ARMENTIÈRES through ERQUINGHEM revealed large craters at all cross roads and filled parties to commence clearing the road. A party of men was at once sent to commence clearing operations. A footbridge at H.4.C.1.5 was completed at 17.00.	3.um
	3rd		Work commenced on filling in and making working parties of craters in the ERQUINGHEM main road and the passage of lorries was made possible by 18.00 hrs same evening.	Appendix	4.um 5.um
	4th 5th		Work on road continued	Appendix "A" 1 Officer 196 OR	9.um

Army Form C. 2118.

WAR DIARY
or
INTELLIGENCE SUMMARY.
(Erase heading not required.)

(2) Continued OCTOBER 1918

Instructions regarding War Diaries and Intelligence Summaries are contained in F. S. Regs., Part II. and the Staff Manual respectively. Title pages will be prepared in manuscript.

Place	Date	Hour	Summary of Events and Information	Remarks and references to Appendices
A16A73	6th		Set to top of H.5.c.0.7.1 above heavy traffic confused	S.L.W.
	7th		The road from the pontoon bridge to CAPPELLE D'ARMENTIERES passable for heavy traffic. The company becomes Reserve Company and is responsible for (a) maintenance of road bridge west of ARMENTIERES (b) Road west of railway crossing at H.6.a.0.9 (c) Access to bank area	S.L.W.
			Major R.T. Jukes R.E. proceeds to ⟨…⟩ ⟨…⟩ Corps Officers Rest hotel at BOULOGNE for an trade and bridge attempted continued	S.L.W.
	8th		Work on trade and bridge attempted continued	S.L.W.
	9th		O.C. left company to proceed on 28 days special leave to England. Sept. Ashworth, R.E. took over command of the company	P.M.
	10th		Work consists of building access halls at STEENWERCK and ERQUINGHEM, Baths, dont Pelaton and foot Cleansing Centres	P.M.
	11th		work continued	P.M.
	12th		work continued	P.M.
	13th		On section moved with ⟨Divisional⟩ ARMENTIERES and commenced work on new Divisional Headquarters	P.M.

WAR DIARY
INTELLIGENCE SUMMARY.

(Erase heading not required.)

Army Form C. 2118.

Continued (3)

Place	Date	Hour	Summary of Events and Information	Remarks and references to Appendices
A.16.d.3.3.	14th		the Trestle at STEENWERCK completed and opened as required	J.M.
	15th		Work in Divisional Area continued	R.M.
B.30.c.14.	16th		No 2 section moved into ARMENTIERES & to help with work in Div H.Q. The rest of the company & Mess Transport moved to B.30.c.14. here to Para 7 R3 received company from leave.	R.M.
	17th	2½ hour	S.JULIEN proceeded a lime to MK On second bridge, enemy's withdrawal. The company in places in a state of readiness to proceed forward at once. War Section moved forward to J.8.d.65.05.	R.M.
	18th			R.M.
T.8.d.65.05	19th		War bridges erected forward in advance of J.8.d.65.05 at J.8.6.2. and J.1.a.15.10	R.M.
PERENCHIES	20		The company moved to J.8.d.65.05. on 19th. Strength of Company 7 Offs. 209 O.R.	R.M.
	21		Cooks filled and roads cleared. Rail head proceeds a lime at Black	R.M.
	22.		Roads + Rly in this area in state for inspection and training	R.M.
K.2.4.8.0	23		The company moved to K.2.b.8.0. Burning the huts finding the transport has been extensive in recovering positions and looting up equipment to MOTTEAUX where	R.M.
WAMBRECHIES			a shelter is being made.	R.M.

WAR DIARY
or
INTELLIGENCE SUMMARY.
(Erase heading not required.)

Army Form C. 2118.

Place	Date	Hour	Summary of Events and Information	Remarks and references to Appendices
WATEROUCHIES 36/I A.2.b.8.0	24		Company training, refitting etc.	R.Y.
	25		"	R.Y.
	26		Warning order received that the Battalion would relieve the 21st Division in the line	R.Y.
LYS-LEZ-LANNOY 37/G.4.d.8.2	27		The Battalion moved to LYS-LEZ-LANNOY and are billeted in a farm and outbuildings	R.Y.
	28		Part of the Cookers collapsed on arriving at 37/A.29.d.b.3	R.Y.
			Three kitchens removed from Moureux to 29 Field Company RE at NECHIN, the remainder for repair to RE R. ESCAULT.	R.Y.
	29		Bridge completed. A forward dump is being formed by this Company at H.B.A. in Company in readiness for forming cartridges in readiness for the crossing of the R. ESCAULT.	R.Y.
	30		A blank on ground at A.29.d.1.9	R.Y.
	31		A bridge at A.27.d.1.9 and the canal the R. MARCK for an addition of 4 lines started.	R.Y.

Chandhour Capt R.E.
O.C. 141 Fd Co R.E.

CONFIDENTIAL

WD 30

224 Field Coy. R.E

Nov. 1918

Vol: 30

WAR DIARY

Capt Crowthers
22 May 1824
R.y.

Army Form C. 2118.

WAR DIARY
or
INTELLIGENCE SUMMARY.

(Erase heading not required.)

November 1918.

Instructions regarding War Diaries and Intelligence Summaries are contained in F. S. Regs., Part II. and the Staff Manual respectively. Title pages will be prepared in manuscript.

Place	Date	Hour	Summary of Events and Information	Remarks and references to Appendices
LYS-LES-LANNOY 57/G.4.d.8.2	1st		The company is employed on making a dump of bridging material at H.3.A. (in NECHIN) in preparation for crossing the R. ESCAUT. Bermon floats which have been ordered being repaired.	2 Rnn
	2nd		Coy. commenced strengthening and rebuilding bridge over ROUBAIX Canal. Effective strength 20 Y Officers : 203 OR	2 Rnn
	3rd		Work on bridge and preparation of dump continues	2 Rnn
	4th		"	2 Rnn
	5th		"	
	6th		Captain J. Strathmore R.E. joined the Company from R.E. Base Depot & relieves Captain A. Graham R.E. who has been appointed to the command of the 62nd Field Company R.E.	2 Rnn
	7th		Work continues	2 Rnn
	8th		At about noon R.E. proceed to No. 62 Field Coy from R.E. as Officer commanding myself & Captain W.C R.E. appears company from here and assume command of the Company. German whereabouts opposite division front commenced during incorrect of the 8th.	2 Rnn
	9th		Notice received from O.C. 209 Field Coy R.E. at 05.30 hrs that withdrawal has commenced. Company held in readiness & ordered forward immediately. Work commenced in Le RUAGE Pont from PECR. Effective strength Y. 202.	2 Rnn

WAR DIARY or INTELLIGENCE SUMMARY

Army Form C. 2118.

November 1918.

Place	Date	Hour	Summary of Events and Information	Remarks and references to Appendices
PETIT LANNOY (nr. PECQ) C.25.d.1.1.	10th		Company moved to PETIT LANNOY near PECQ, and is employed in forward roads, watering areas etc.	Pecq
	11th		Cessation of hostilities at 11.00 hours.	
	12th		Work on roads and communications continued	
	13th		"	
	14th		On movement of 279 and 231 Field Companies from the area, this century took over the completion of 231 the Coy's bridge at WARCOING and the maintenance of all bridges of or in the environs.	
	15th		Attached Infantry rejoined Two units G.H.Q.	
	16th		Effective strength Y officers: 202 O.R.	
	17th		Throughout services are employed in the Army Communication at ROUBAIX.	
	18th		Company represented by 12 O.R. took a share and took a share and took in and took in columns.	
	19th		C.R.E. and O.C. was to inspect WARCOING and HERRINES with a view to handing Reconnaissance of R. ESCAUT made.	
	20th		Work on returning WARCOING and HERRINES and returning Bourron	

Army Form C. 2118.

WAR DIARY
or
INTELLIGENCE SUMMARY.
(Erase heading not required.)

(3)

November 1916

Place	Date	Hour	Summary of Events and Information	Remarks and references to Appendices
HERINNES 37/c 21.b.5.8.	21		Company moved to HERINNES and is employed rebuilding partially demolished houses.	
"	22		Effective strength 1 offr. 200 ORs. Company employed rebuilding & repairing houses damaged by shell fire and clearing debris from villain near RR bridge at WARCOING.	
"	23		— ditto —	
"	24		— ditto —	
"	25		— ditto —	
"	26		Lieut G. A. black M.C. N.E. rejoined unit from leave to UK.	
"	27		Company employed rebuilding & repairing houses damaged by shell fire & clearing debris from R.R. bridge at WARCOING.	
"	28		— ditto —	
"	29		— ditto —	
"	30		— ditto —	

E. R. Martin Major R.E.
OC 22nd Field Coy R.E.

CONFIDENTIAL.

WAR DIARY.

224 FIELD COMPANY, R.E.

FROM :- 1st Dec. 1918
TO :- 31st Dec. 1918

VOLUME No 31.

Army Form C. 2118.

WAR DIARY
or
INTELLIGENCE SUMMARY.
(Erase heading not required.)

DECEMBER 1918.

Instructions regarding War Diaries and Intelligence Summaries are contained in F. S. Regs., Part II. and the Staff Manual respectively. Title pages will be prepared in manuscript.

Place	Date	Hour	Summary of Events and Information	Remarks and references to Appendices
HERINNES. 37/c.21.6.58.	1st		Company employed in rebuilding demolished houses and clearing debris from the R. ESCAUT and WARCOING bridge.	—
PETIT BAISSIEUX	2nd		Company moved to PETIT BAISSIEUX for work in progress of War Cage. The majority of the company billeted in 150 tenting.	—
	3rd		Lieut K.S. Stobie evacuated to Base sick.	—
	4th		Croix de Guerre (French with Silver Star) awarded to Cpl A Beaulieu R2 (late P.Co. inf.) now commanding 62nd Field Co REF and Croix de Guerre (with bronze star) awarded to N°44024 Sapper A. Rayo.	—
	5th			—
	6		Work in progress of War Cage continued — difficulty experienced in getting material.	—
	7th		Effective strength Y Officers 361 OR	—
	8th			—
	9		Work on P.o.W. Cage continued.	—
	13th		Effective strength 7 Officers 199 OR	—
	14th			—
	15th		Work continues	—
	16			—
	17th		Some preparations made and work for demobilisation	—
	18th			—
	19		Work continues	—
	20			—

WAR DIARY
or
INTELLIGENCE SUMMARY.

(Erase heading not required.)

Army Form C. 2118.

Instructions regarding War Diaries and Intelligence Summaries are contained in F.S. Regs., Part II. and the Staff Manual respectively. Title pages will be prepared in manuscript.

Continued.

Place	Date	Hour	Summary of Events and Information	Remarks and references to Appendices
PETIT BAISSIEUX	21st		Effective strength 9 officers 194 OR	
	22nd		Orders received to cease all work on the Proposed f. War Camp.	
	23rd			
	24th		Company employed in training & onto aerodrome site	
	25th		Whole holidays. Concert f. Wheat Drive arranged for Xmas night	
	26th		4 new F.C. Rolling kitchens joined Company from R.E. Base Depot	
	27th		Training continued	
	28th			
	29th		Effective strength 9 officers 192 OR	
	30th			
	31st		Training continued	

E.L. Martin
O.C. 224TH FIELD COY. ROYAL ENGINEERS.

Army Form W.3091.

Cover for Documents.

CONFIDENTIAL.

Nature of Enclosures.

WAR DIARY

OF

224 FIELD COY R.E.

FROM:- 1st JAN 1919.

TO:- 31st JAN 1919.

VOLUME 32.

Notes, or Letters written.

Army Form C. 2118.

WAR DIARY
or
INTELLIGENCE SUMMARY.
(Erase heading not required.)

JANUARY 1919.

Place	Date	Hour	Summary of Events and Information	Remarks and references to Appendices
PETIT	1.		Company employed in Company, etc. including football and games.	
BAISIEUX	2		Major G.E. Marks M.C. R.E. 2 I/C A/CRE during absence of OCRE a leave.	
			Cadre shortcourse for Commanders of the Company.	
57/M.9.d.7.6.	3		Training and games continued	
	4		Special Church Service 1830 OR	
	5			
	6			
	7			
	8			
	9		Training and Games continued	
	10			
	11			
	12		Effective strength 8 officers 163 OR	
	13			
	14			
	15		Training cont.	
	16		Cdr R.E. Lt 2/Lt H.G. attached to D.A.D. Lt W.E. [?] Army	
	17		Capt. 2/Lt Thorpe M.C. RE proceeded to SN.2 Division	
			returned from PZ Leave and assumed duty the Company	
	18		Effective Strength 6 Officers and 180 OR	
			2/Lieut S. Jack R.E. proceeded U.K. for demobilisation	
	19			
	20		Training and games continued	
	21			

Army Form C. 2118.

WAR DIARY
or
INTELLIGENCE SUMMARY.

(Erase heading not required.)

Instructions regarding War Diaries and Intelligence Summaries are contained in F. S. Regs., Part II. and the Staff Manual respectively. Title pages will be prepared in manuscript.

Continued

Place	Date	Hour	Summary of Events and Information	Remarks and references to Appendices
PETIT BAISIEUX 37/M,N,9.d.7.6	22 23 24		Training and games continued	A.P. A.P.
	25		Orders received to take over work on the Halte Repos, Basieux Station	A.P.
	26 27		Work on Halte Repos continued. The chief work consists of erecting storehouses and a new dining room for officers. now to 30 Ruinwalling Cy R.E	A.P. A.P.
	28		Orders received to discontinue work on the Halte Repos and to be prepared to move tomorrow	A.P.
CROIX 36/L.q.b.05.35	29 30 31		Company moved to billets in Croix Company engaged chiefly on billet improvements. The detachts hunted personnel mite goes as far as possible for supper.	A.P. A.P. A.P.

[signature]
Lieut R.E.
O.C. 224 Field Coy R.E.

SECRET

WAR DIARY

224 FIELD COMPANY, R.E.

FEBRUARY 1919.   VOL. 29

Army Form C. 2118.

WAR DIARY
or
INTELLIGENCE SUMMARY.
(Erase heading not required.)

FEBRUARY 1919.

Instructions regarding War Diaries and Intelligence Summaries are contained in F. S. Regs., Part II. and the Staff Manual respectively. Title pages will be prepared in manuscript.

Place	Date	Hour	Summary of Events and Information	Remarks and references to Appendices
CROIX 51/4.9.6.05.25	1st		The Company is in bivouac opposite Neufchyten. All open billets - cavalry.	—
	2nd		231 Field Company in Croix. 7 Railway bridge in Neufchyten.	—
	3rd		Work continued. Lieut Engler R.E. M.C. proceeded home for Demobilization. (T.2)	—
	4th		O.C. issues new 2nd orders for work — new conditions of billets.	—
	5th		Major E.C. Martin M.C. R.E. depart from Effective Command and received Command of 94.	—
	6th		2/Lt ___ appointed as 2nd officer of 4th Section in 2nd Lt Giles R.E.	—
	7th		2nd Lt C. Hunt R.E. proceeded U.K. for Demobilization.	—
	8th		Lieut Littlewood attended Armament Course for P.E.	—
			2nd Lieut G.E. ___ and D.M. Bruce of R.E. Group arrived. O.C. 3rd Section Cpl E___. Effective strength of 264 Co 3 officers, 115 O.R.	—
	9th		Weather remains too cold for concrete. 2 officers Demobilization for are inclusive of above.	—
	10th		Work on Bridge continued by all available labour.	—
	11th			—
	12th		Movement O.R.C. reporting strike. Only stone taken and Razors fuel.	—
	13th			
	14th			—
	15th		Work continued on Bridge. Effective strength of Co. 2 officers 104 O.R.	—
	16th		Work continued on Bridge and on Path at Marbriches.	—
	17th		Lt J.A. Kennedy R.E. + 2/Lt J.C. Brown R.E. transferred to the Co. from 231 247 Cos.	—
	18th		Work on Bridge continued.	—
	19th			—
	20th			—

Army Form C. 2118.

WAR DIARY
or
INTELLIGENCE SUMMARY.

(Erase heading not required.)

FEBRUARY 1919.

Place	Date	Hour	Summary of Events and Information	Remarks and references to Appendices
CROIX 36/L.9&025	21		Work continued on Bridge Baths	aan
	22		Effective Strength 4 Officers 100 OR	aan
	23		Work on Bridge Continued	aan
	24		Nominal Roll of Cadres sent to R.D. for Chainery Bowie. Work continued	aen
	25		Work on Bridge Continued. Repair of Baths at Wambrechies completed	aen
	26		Work on Bridge continued	9 km
	27		Baths at WAMBRECHIES reported in need of slight repair. Sappers sent to do the work	9 km
	28		Effective Strength of Co. 4 Offrs 99 OR.	

S.L. Marten
Major RE
O/C 224 Field Company R.E.

SECRET

224th Field Co. R.E.

WAR DIARY

March 1919   Vol. 34

WAR DIARY
or
INTELLIGENCE SUMMARY.
(Erase heading not required.)

Army Form C. 2118.

MARCH 1919

Place	Date	Hour	Summary of Events and Information	Remarks and references to Appendices
CROIX 36/L9 d.052	1st		Repair of Baths at Wasnechies completed. Work continues on Bridge at Roubaix	S.W
	2nd		Major Hurley M.C., R.E. O.C. Company Proceeded on Leave Capt J.H. Wood R.E. assuming Command	S.W
	3rd		Work on Bridge continues	S.W
	4th			
	5th		31 O.R. from 231 Fd.Co. R.E. transferred to 234 Fd.Co. R.E. but now attached to 231 Fd.Co.R.E. 4 O.R. from 2nd and 3rd Corps transferred to 231 Fd.Co.R.E	S.W
	6th		Work on bridge continues	
	7th			S.W
	8th		Effective Strength 4 Officers 126 O.R	
	9th			S.W
	10th		Work continued on the bridge	S.W
	11th		Exchange of Bridge completed. Repairs carried out at "A" & "Q" Clerks Offices Examination of 13 huts at Roubaix for use as billets for Company. Small kit deliveries also carried out	S.W
	12th		All available Sappers cleaning barrack etc	
	13th		Work started on erection of New Divisional Baths at ROUBAIX	
	14th		Lt J.A. Kennedy R.E. joined Co on completion of Agricultural Course	S.W
	15th		Effective strength 4 Officers 118 O.R	
	16th		Orders from Division received that 2Lt Fassmore & 2Lt Mills being struck off strength from 14.3.19. Capt H.S Renard R.E transferred to 2nd 1st Do	
	17th		Work continued on new Baths. Capt H.S Renard R.E transferred to 2nd 1st Div from 22.3.19. Proceeded on leave 17th	
	18th		Work continued on Baths	
	19th		Erection of further huts started	

Army Form C. 2118.

WAR DIARY
or
INTELLIGENCE SUMMARY.

March 1919 (continued)

(Erase heading not required.)

Place	Date	Hour	Summary of Events and Information	Remarks and references to Appendices
CROIX	20		Major E.A. Pasley M.C. R.E. relinquished command of Coy on appointment as O.C. 438 Field Coy R.E. 3rd Division	
	21		Party went to TEMPLEUVE to unsaddle Horses & Stores	
	22		38 OR employed to Castre "A" Coy R.E. for Transport. Effective strength 4 officers 70 OR	JY
	23		Routine	
	24		Dismantling of 73 SE at TEMPLEUVE completed	
	25		Routine	
	26			
	27		Capt A.B Rayner R.E joined the Company from DADG RE, Fifth Army. Assumed Command	aRR
	28		Routine. Effective strength 2 officers 70 OR	aRR
	29		Routine	aRR
	30		O.C.'s inspection of Tools, Carts, Clothing & Equipment	aRR
	31		Effective strength 2 off 10 OR	

A.B Rayner. Capt RE.
O.C. 224 Field Coy R.E.

SECRET

WR 35

224th Field Co. R.E.

60Div

War Diary

Vol. 35

March 1919.

April

Army Form C. 2118.

WAR DIARY
INTELLIGENCE SUMMARY.
(Erase heading not required.)

224 Field Coy RE. APRIL 1919.

Place	Date	Hour	Summary of Events and Information	Remarks and references to Appendices
CROIX 36/1: q & 05 25	1st		O.C. continued Inspection of Tool Carts & GS Waggon Stores	AB
	2nd		Routine	AB
	3rd		Inspection of Saddlery & G.S. Equipment by O.C	O32
	4th		Routine	AB
	5th		Parade. Effective strength 2 officers 67 O.R.	AB
	6th		Routine	AB
	7th		All available men cleaning & oiling	AB
	8th		Company in Billets. Inspection by O.C.	AB
	9th		Cleaning of Saddlery continued	AB
	10th		Routine	AB
	11th		Routine	AB
	12th		Routine. Effective strength 2 officers 68 O.R.	AB
	13th		Company attended Divine Service at Drill Hall & marched past L.O.C.	AB
	14th		Work commenced on drawing surface water at Hall's Repair, Review, 1 NCO from Co. Supervising	AB
	15th		Routine	AB
	16th		Routine	AB
	17th		Good Friday. No duty.	AB
	18th			AB
	19th		Routine. Effective strength 2 officers 67 O.R.	AB

Army Form C. 2118.

WAR DIARY
or
INTELLIGENCE SUMMARY.
(Erase heading not required.)

224 Field C.R.E.   APRIL 1919 (cont)

Place	Date	Hour	Summary of Events and Information	Remarks and references to Appendices
CROIX 36/Lg & 05.25	20th		~~Parade~~ Divisional Church Parade	
	21st		First Parade of Vehicle Guard at Brigade Guard mounting. Later Roberts to remainder	AR
	22nd		Routine	
	23rd		}	AR
	24th			AR
	25th			
	26th		Routine. Effective Strength 2 Officers 66 O.R.	AR
	27th		Divisional Church Parade.	AR
	28th		Annual Strength reduced to minimum of 2 L.D. Horses.	AR
	29th		Routine	AR
	30th		Routine. Effective strength 2 Officers 65 O.R.	AR

A.R. Rayner
Capt. R.E.
O.C. 224 Field Co. R.E.

www.ingramcontent.com/pod-product-compliance
Lightning Source LLC
Chambersburg PA
CBHW080906230426
43664CB00016B/2735